P9-DYE-073

Partnering with Purpose

Z716,4
,C76
2004

Partnering with Purpose

A Guide to Strategic Partnership Development for Libraries and Other Organizations

Janet L. Crowther

Barry Trott

LIBRARIES UNLIMITED

A Member of the Greenwood Publishing Group

Westport, Connecticut • London

Library of Congress Cataloging-in-Publication Data

Crowther, Janet L.
    Partnering with purpose : a guide to strategic partnership development for libraries and other organizations / Janet L. Crowther and Barry Trott.
        p. cm.
    Includes bibliographical references and index.
    ISBN 1-59158-090-0 (pbk. : alk. paper)
    1. Libraries and community. 2. Libraries and business. 3. Public-private sector cooperation. 4. Partnerships. 5. Libraries—Public relations. I. Trott, Barry, 1961- II. Title.
Z716.4.C76   2004
021.2—dc22   2004048641

British Library Cataloguing in Publication Data is available.

Library of Congress Catalog Card Number: 2004048641
ISBN: 1-59158-090-0

First published in 2004

Libraries Unlimited, 88 Post Road West, Westport, CT 06881
A Member of the Greenwood Publishing Group, Inc.
www.lu.com

Printed in the United States of America

∞™

The paper used in this book complies with the Permanent Paper Standard issued by the National Information Standards Organization (Z39.48-1984).

10 9 8 7 6 5 4 3 2 1

To Jean Preer, for introducing me to the excitement and possibilities of librarianship

—Barry

To Helen Clendennin

—Janet

Contents

Acknowledgments

Janet and Barry would like to thank the following people, without whom this book could not have been written: John Moorman and Patsy Hansel, who as library directors had the vision to see partnering as an important tool for the Williamsburg Regional Library; our management colleagues at WRL, who have taken up the challenge of partnership development as a strategic direction; the partnership managers at the library, whose hard work and passion are responsible for the success of our community partnerships; and the staff at WRL, who support partnering with their ideas, skills, and time.

We would also like to thank our community partners for their energy, enthusiasm, and excitement. Their willingness to work collaboratively with the library has made our community a richer place.

Finally, thanks go to our families—Lynn and Eleanor Trott and Jim, Ben, and Seth Heller—for all of their support during this project.

Introduction

As libraries head into the twenty-first century, they face increasing pressures. Budget reductions, staff cuts, increasing materials costs, and the challenges presented by the Internet and electronic information all require libraries to look at new patterns for providing service to their communities. One model that has come to the forefront over the past decade is using partnerships to strengthen the library's position. The Williamsburg Regional Library has been active in developing and promoting partnering as a tool for success in libraries. We have established thriving relationships with a variety of local institutions. We partner with the Sentara Williamsburg Community Hospital to host a cancer resource center and to promote consumer health in our community. Our partnership with the Colonial National Historical Park has led to the development of our award-winning Park Pack program that lets library patrons check out a backpack of materials to enrich their experience when exploring our local national parks. Our partnership with the local public schools has been used as a model by a task force on school/library cooperation set up by the Library of Virginia and the Virginia Educational Media Association. We have found through discussion with colleagues and through presentations at state and national conferences that there is an interest in the concept of partnering and a demand in the profession for a guide for libraries of all sizes (not just large urban systems) that discusses and illustrates how to establish and sustain a partnering program in the library. Hence this book.

Over the years, libraries have always developed relationships with organizations in their communities. Frequently though, the work that the libraries have done—commitment of staff time and resources, purchasing of materials, etc.—has not been recognized. By developing formalized partnerships with these community groups, libraries can be recognized for the value that they bring to their communities. In addition, community partnership development can become an important strategic tool for expanding library resources, gaining new users, and building community support for the library.

The word "partnership" has been used in a variety of ways, and even within the library community there are myriad examples of programs that are defined as partnerships. *Partnering with Purpose* is a process-oriented book. It does not attempt to be academic in its approach to partnership development, and it is not research-based. Building on the success of the Williamsburg Regional Library model for partnership development, it gives libraries a working definition of what partnering is and enlarges on that beginning to start a dialog in the library profession that will lead to a commonly understood language of partnering. A common understanding of how partnering works, and what it can do for libraries, will enable institutions to approach partnership development in a strategic and librarywide fashion rather than piecemeal.

Partnering is a tool, not an end in itself. This book explores, in a very practical way, how you can develop and manage partnerships within your library. We examine and discuss setting up the organizational structure for partnership development in the library, exploring the community for potential partners, establishing and formalizing a partnership, managing ongoing relationships, evaluating partnering efforts, and dealing with potential problems in partnering. Throughout the book, we include examples of collaborative efforts that we have developed at our library, and we include samples of documents and forms that have been useful to us in the process.

Partnership development is by no means limited to public libraries. All types of libraries can take advantage of the processes and procedures outlined in this book. Nonprofit organizations will also find useful information here on how they can use partnering as a strategic direction to support their mission. Because we feel that partnership development is most successful when taken on in an organizationwide fashion, we have aimed much of the material in the book at those people who are decision makers in their institutions—library directors, administrators, department heads, and trustees. Without support from these levels, it is hard to have a successful partnering program. However, if you approach partnering in a strategic, librarywide fashion, it will be an important tool for promoting your library's importance in its community.

Partnering with Purpose

1

What Is Partnering?

A partnership is:

- A voluntary association of two or more persons who jointly own and carry on a business for profit. Cf. Joint venture; strategic alliance. (*Black's Law Dictionary*)[1]

- A contract between two or more people in a joint business who agree to pool their funds and talent and share in the profits and losses of the enterprise. (*Dictionary of Finance and Investment Terms*)[2]

- The fact or condition of being a partner; association or participation. 1576 Fleming Panopl. Epist. 23. (*Oxford English Dictionary*)[3]

- 1. The state of being a partner: participation. 2. a: a legal relation existing between two or more persons contractually associated as joint principals in a business b: the persons joined together in a partnership. 3. a relationship resembling a legal partnership and usually involving close cooperation between parties having specified and joint rights and responsibilities. (*Merriam-Webster's Collegiate Dictionary*)[4]

A (Very) Brief History of Partnering

Looking at the historical record, the words "partnership" and "partnership development" started to appear in the business literature in the 1970s. At this time, and throughout much of the 1980s, the drive to develop partnerships was initiated in business schools. Shortly thereafter, businesses drove the efforts. As Shirley Sagawa and Eli Segal point out in *Common Interest, Common Good: Creating Value Through Business and Social Sector Partnerships*, businesses were actively seeking out opportunities to form "strategic alliances" with other for-profit organizations by the early 1980s.[5] The driving force behind these partnerships was the desire to reach out to customers in new ways and to make better use of resources through joint ventures.

At that time, the nonprofit sector had not begun to explore partnering in any major way. In fact, as Sagawa and Segal note, nonprofit America evidenced a strong distrust of new ideas coming from the business sector at this time. The fear of being co-opted by for-profit organizations was high among nonprofits, and many nonprofits were wary of corporate motives for wanting to build alliances. These concerns, still evident today, should be taken into account when looking at developing a partnership with a for-profit organization, but should not be a factor in limiting library partnering opportunities to only other nonprofit organizations.

During the 1980s, businesses began to restructure and downsize, and part of this reprioritization involved a review of corporate giving policies and traditions. Up to this point, businesses had been giving increasingly large sums of money to the nonprofit sector, and by the mid-1980s, corporate giving to nonprofits had exceeded foundation giving.[6] In exchange for this largesse, most corporations and businesses had been willing to accept name recognition and building a better community image.

As money grew increasingly tight in the 1980s, businesses sought more tangible returns for their corporate giving plans. More businesses began to utilize "cause-related marketing"—giving funds to nonprofits based on customer transactions. For every dollar spent with Company X, that company would give a percentage to Nonprofit Group Y. This interest in the corporate community in restructuring their philanthropic efforts was the opening move in developing a dialog between the for-profit and nonprofit sectors about the possibilities offered by strategic partnerships. Since the 1990s, the move in corporate giving increasingly has shifted away from pure donations toward building relationships that can benefit both the giver and the receiver.

As businesses and nonprofit groups began to build relationships based on corporate giving, they began to realize that both for-profit and nonprofit organizations could look beyond their own sectors for solutions to issues and problems. In his 2001 article on partnering in arts development, Alvin Reiss noted the successful partnership between the St. Louis (MO) Symphony and thirty local black churches. This relationship led to increased African American attendance at symphony events and helped to establish the symphony as "a concerned partner in the community."[7] Similarly, Michael Anft discusses the collaboration between General Motors and the nonprofit environmental organization the Tellus Institute that allowed GM to "curb its use of chemicals by 30 percent at its 60 North American factories, thus saving the company tens of millions of dollars since then and giving GM an accomplishment it could cite when its environmental record was criticized."[8]

Throughout the last decade of the twentieth century and the first several years of the twenty-first, the trend in partnering has been for organizations to look for partners unlike themselves—business and nonprofit, nonprofit and government (federal, state, and local), business and government, etc. The success of early versions of these cross-cultural partnerships has provided models for continued efforts along these lines. In addition, significant forces are driving the partnership model in both the public and private sectors.

In *The Collaborative Challenge: How Non-profits and Businesses Succeed Through Strategic Alliances*, James Austin identifies forces in three particular areas that fuel the formation of cross-sector partnerships from the public or nonprofit sector:[9]

1. Political forces: Austin notes that since the presidency of Ronald Reagan in the 1980s, the role and the size of the government, in particular the federal government, have been changing radically. Each administration since that time has embraced the idea that the federal government should not be the leader in addressing social problems. There has been a consistent shifting of responsibilities for social issues, in terms of both funds and staffing, from the federal government to state and local governments, and to community-based nonprofit and religious organizations. At the same time there has been a consistent challenge to the private sector to become involved in dealing with social issues and to look for market-based solutions to social problems.

2. Economic forces: Government funding for nonprofits has become increasingly scarce as political pressures for leaner budgets and balanced budgets have resonated throughout all levels of government. Previously, the federal government had been one of the largest funders of nonprofit

organizations, but decreasing federal funding has forced nonprofits to seek new sources of revenue. Frequently, this search has led nonprofits to develop partnerships with businesses and state and local governments to survive.

3.   Social forces: Another driving force in the move toward collaboration is the realization that the social problems faced by the nation and by individual communities are too complex for a single entity to deal with. Health care, education, poverty, and the like are problems that can best be addressed through collaboration across sectors: government, business, and nonprofit. Examples of this cross-sector partnering to deal with social concerns during the 1990s include President Clinton's Americorp initiative, which brought the business community and the federal government together under the theme of "building communities through cross-sector partnering"; and President G.W. Bush's "faith-based initiatives," which encouraged churches to work with the federal government in addressing a host of social issues.

In *Working Across Boundaries: Making Collaboration Work in Government and Nonprofit Organizations,* Russell Linden identifies an additional force behind the trend. Based on over two decades of experience leading management education programs for public and nonprofit managers and leaders, Linden has witnessed an increase in understanding and acceptance by managers of the importance of collaboration. Linden hopes that with this increased understanding of cross-sector collaboration will lead to more successful models of cooperation within communities.[10]

Libraries are not exempt from forces in the community that create both the expectation and the opportunity for partnership development. Local funding bodies are looking at library budgets and encouraging libraries to reach out into the community in new ways. Library budgets are constantly under the close scrutiny of funding agencies, and cross-sector collaboration may also be a mechanism for libraries to both supplement funding as well as enhance their reputation as responsible stewards of public funds.

Partnerships can also be a mechanism for libraries not only to address traditional issues, such as literacy, but also to become more integrated into their community's organizational structure. As outcome-based evaluation becomes an increasingly common tool in deciding on funding priorities, partnerships offer the library the possibility of working with organizations that have mechanisms in place to track outcomes.

Organizations seeking to develop partnerships must consider the question, "What motivates each of the sectors to form strategic partnerships with other types of entities?" While business, nonprofits, and governments all share certain motivations for partnering, it is useful to understand what in particular motivates each group.

Businesses

- Strategic gains

    – Increased credibility in the community

    – Goodwill

- Greater access to key customer groups, new business opportunities, and expanded markets

- Access to unique resources

- Access to community leaders

- More immediate return for an investment (as opposed to simply making a monetary donation)

- Staff development opportunities

    – Attract, motivate, and retain staff through greater participation

    – Keep staff focused on service

- May be part of the business's mission:

  - Ben and Jerry's, Home Depot, and other corporations have community focus as part of their corporate values

- Quicker response to competitive pressures through well-crafted alliances

Nonprofits

- Supplement declining revenues

- Increased emphasis on results

  - Outcome-based measurements force organizations to think and work collaboratively

- Grant funding often requires, or at least rewards, collaboration

- Expands access into the community

- Increases the organization's visibility in the community

- Cost savings

- Collaboration is necessary to stay relevant or even to survive

- Reinforce the organization's leadership role in the community

- Maintain a positive community image

Governments

- Bolster decreasing budgets

- Access to difficult-to-reach parts of the community

- Access to specialized knowledge of potential partners

- Expand resources in light of decreasing size of the government workforce

- Political mandates to collaborate with other organizations

- Establish leadership within community on specific issues

- Maintain a positive community image

Libraries and Partnering

Libraries have made good use of collaborative relationships with other libraries throughout their history. Projects such as OCLC's collaborative cataloging, interlibrary loan, and a wide range of consortial arrangements demonstrate the interest and ability of libraries to come together to develop new products and services.

Joint school/public libraries, with elementary, secondary, and college partners, have been and continue to be the result of libraries working together in a formal way to make the best use of resources. Collective purchasing of materials and group purchases of access to online resources in both the public and academic library sectors again shows that libraries are willing and able to work collaboratively with similar organizations.

This trend continues today as the profession explores ways to collaborate in the provision of reference services through such projects as the joint OCLC/Library of Congress QuestionPoint service and other similar initiatives. The virtual library movement has also been a driving force in promoting collaboration between libraries to develop new means of serving users. However, with some notable exceptions, most libraries have not extended this model of collaboration beyond working in partnership with other libraries. Libraries have been slow to pick up on the value and necessity of cross-sector partnering.

Libraries have, of course, devoted energy to achieving their goals by working with other entities, but many of what are described in the professional literature as library partnerships reflect something less than a true marriage of equals, whose gains and risks are mutually shared by the partners. Rather, what is often described as "partnering" more typically involves libraries adding or developing resources and then promoting those resources through community organizations. While promoting library resources and services is essential to the success of the organization, it should not be confused with building partnerships through which the library can not only market its resources and services but also receive some tangible, measurable return from its investment in the partnership.

Typical of some of these types of projects is the National Partners for Libraries and Literacy program, developed by the American Library Association in the mid-1980s as a mechanism to promote library literacy efforts and "increase community support for [libraries]." ALA developed links with sixty-one national organizations whose missions included reading and literacy. Libraries were then encouraged to work with the local and regional branches of these organizations to promote libraries and literacy. The Partners program provided a variety of suggestions for how libraries can connect with local organizations: looking for shared interests, promoting library resources to partners, developing collections of interest to partner organizations, offering technical assistance to partners, providing information referral services, etc.[11] Although libraries would certainly benefit from this sort of promotional program, this project is better described as a library marketing effort rather than a true partnership.

In the library community, there have been calls since the early 1990s for increased participation in the community through partnering. In 1993, Susan Goldberg called on libraries to "plan for services that anticipate changes rather than react to them."[12] In her article, Goldberg develops a concept of connecting circles of leadership in both the library and the community. Within the library there are the library board, the director, the management team, the staff, the Friends of the Library, and others. In the community, the leadership circles can be found in the elected officials, funding bodies, and community leadership groups. Goldberg cites the importance of connecting these two groups of leadership circles to solidify the role of the library within the community.

Although she does not specifically mention the idea of formal partnerships, Goldberg's analysis of the importance of connecting the library with the community leaders reflects one of the foundations for partnership development: working through gatekeepers in the community to reach broader audiences. Goldberg seeks to strengthen the library's role in the community and its role as a community partner by including the community in the library decision-making process.

Another advocate for the importance of partnership development in public libraries has been the Urban Libraries Council. Founded in 1971, the ULC brings together "the trustees, library directors, and corporate officers of member institutions [to] work together to address shared issues, grasp new opportunities, and conduct research that improves professional practice."[13] In 1997, the ULC produced a publication titled *Leading the Way: Partnering for Success* (1997), and more recently published *Partnerships for Free Choice Learning: Public Libraries, Museums and Public Broadcasters Working Together* (available at http://www.urbanlibraries.org/standards/research.html). Both of these publications discuss how partnering can benefit urban libraries and look at potential partners in a variety of sectors. *Partnering for Success* includes a very useful statement of partnership goals and objectives. *Partnerships for Free Choice* includes sections on the assets and liabilities of partnerships as well as a discussion of some of the risks associated with partnering.

The most prominent proponent of library partnership development has been Glen E. Holt, director of the St. Louis (Missouri) Public Library (SLPL). Under Holt's leadership, SLPL has actively sought out and established cross-sector partnerships since the late 1980s. In 1999, Holt laid out his concept of the importance of community partnerships for public libraries in "Public Library Partnerships: Mission Driven Tools for 21st Century Success" (http://www.public-libraries.net/en/x_media/pdf/holt6en.pdf). Holt notes that successful partnerships have at their heart "joined self-interest." Holt defines joined self-interest as the situation that exists when "each partner gains more by working with another that by working alone."[14]

At SLPL, formal partnerships have been and continue to be established in a variety of areas defined in Holt's article: training, funding, information dissemination, program development, building and sharing audiences, research partnerships, and political alliances. All of these relationships clearly portray Holt's concept of joint self-interest at work. Holt notes that these relationships have been "a major source of strategic strength for the St. Louis Public Library."[15]

SLPL has not been alone in expanding its reach into the community through partnership development. Other large urban library systems such as Brooklyn (New York) Public Library and Broward County (Florida) Public Library have been active in developing cross-sector partnerships to fulfill the mission of the library. Broward County Library partnerships include a Small Business Resource Center developed in partnership with the Bank of America (http://www.broward.org/sbrc) and The Broward Community Technology Center, formed through a partnership among the Broward County Library, the school board of Broward County, and the South East Florida Library Information Network (http://databases.si. umich.edu/cfdocs/community/helpseek/BPTSDisplay.cfm?topic=Partnerships). The Brooklyn Public Library has partnered with the Brooklyn Art Museum and the Brooklyn Children's Museum to create "Brooklyn Expedition" (http://www.brooklynexpedition.org) to "help young people acquire visual research and technology literacy skills" (http://www.imls.gov/closer/archive/hlt_c0300.htm). The 2004 Library of the Year award was given to the San Jose (California) Public Library and San Jose State University Library in recognition of their shared facility partnership.

Another active promoter of partnerships in the library field has been the Institute of Museum and Library Services (IMLS). IMLS has encouraged collaboration between libraries and other institutions (primarily museums) in a variety of ways. The National Leadership Grants program "supports three funding categories for libraries, three for museums and one for joint library-museum partnerships." The "Model Programs of Library-Museum Collaboration" supports innovative projects that model how museums and libraries can work together to expand their service to the public- with emphasis on serving the community, using technology, or enhancing education" (http://www.imls.gov/grants/library/lib_nlgl.asp). In 1999, the Ann Arbor (Michigan) District Library, the Chicago Public Library, and the Detroit Public Library all received leadership grants supporting partnerships between the library and local museums.[16] More recently, IMLS initiated a partnership with nonprofits, businesses, libraries, and academic institutions to develop the International Children's Library, a collection of digital children's books freely available for children worldwide (http://www. imls.gov/scripts/text.cgi?/whatsnew/02archive/111802.htm). Through its grant programs and other activities, IMLS has been a strong proponent of collaboration for libraries in the United States.

As can be seen from these examples, while the library profession has in some cases moved toward cross-sector partnership development in the past decade, most if not all of the active work in partnership building has come from large libraries, which have visionary leadership and a large pool of resources from which to draw. The question then arises, can small and medium-sized libraries also use partnerships as a tool for achieving their mission and goals? The answer is definitely yes.

It is not necessary for a library to have a large staff or an unlimited pool of funding (something that few if any libraries can claim) to use partnership development as a tool for success. What is needed is a clear vision of what partnering is and the resulting benefits, an understanding of where the library is heading, a commitment from administration to the concept of partnering, and staff buy-in to partnering as a strategic direction. The following chapters describe mechanisms and procedures that allow libraries of any size to develop successful community partnerships to expand the library's reach into the community, build support for the library, develop new resources, and ensure that the library continues to play a central role in the life of its community.

Is Partnering a Fad?

Libraries have seen the coming and going of many management trends. From TQM (total quality management) to self-directed teams, library administrators have tried to put into practice techniques that were first developed in the business sector. All too often, these attempts are applied halfheartedly, in an attempt to convince funders that libraries are on top of current management practices. In many cases, these attempts have no lasting impact on the organization.

So, is partnering just another step in this long line of faddish management practices? We believe that it is not. Management trends are, for the most part, internally focused, and deal with how a particular institution operates. Partnering is external and focused on the community. Since the mission of the public library demands involvement in the community, we think that partnering is and will continue to be an important mechanism by which libraries and other organizations can fulfill their missions now and in the future.

What does seem to be occurring is a shift in emphasis from national-level partnering efforts to more locally based efforts. Partnering will probably continue to happen with increasing frequency at the local level, even if there is a decrease in the emphasis at the national level. What we are experiencing today is part of an ongoing experiment developed by businesses and then taken up by the public sector. Many early examples of partnerships profiled in the 1980s and early 1990s involved high-profile ventures between national organizations and large corporations, such as Microsoft and ALA, Starbucks and Care. What seems more common now are partnerships that focus on more specific markets such as social services, libraries, and environmental organizations. Staff in smaller institutions and smaller communities have looked at the larger trend and are now envisioning how it can be successfully applied at the local level.

The forces mentioned above that drive institutions toward partnership development are unlikely to diminish in the future. Libraries and other organizations will continue look to partnering as a way to support their missions. As partnership development becomes more common in smaller organizations, it will be important for these organizations to remember that partnership development is not an end in itself but an important means to achieving whatever goals the institution has set. The important question to ask is not, "Do partnerships work?" but rather, "What can partnerships achieve?"

Notes

1. (St. Paul, MN: West Group, 1999), 1142.

2. (Haupauge, NY: Barron's Educational Series, 1995), 406.

3. (Oxford: Clarendon Press, 2001), vol. VII, 512.

4. (Springfield, MA: Merriam-Webster, 1993),. 848.

5. Shirley Sagawa and Eli Segal, *Common Interest, Common Good: Creating Value Through Business and Social Sector Partnerships* (Boston: Harvard Business School Press, 2000), xiii.

6. Ibid., 15.

7. Alvin H. Reiss, "Partnerships a Key to Future Arts Development," *Fund Raising Management* 32 (July 2001): 33.

8. Anft, Michael. "Toward Corporate Change." *The Chronicle of Philanthropy* 14 (September 19, 2002): 9.

9. James E. Austin, *The Collaborative Challenge: How Non-profits and Businesses Succeed Through Strategic Alliances* (San Francisco: Jossey-Bass, 2000), 7.

10. Russell M. Linden, *Working Across Boundaries: Making Collaboration Work in Government and Nonprofit Organizations* (San Francisco: Jossey-Bass, 2002), xvi.

11. Mary C. Chobot and Jean Preer, "Partnerships to Promote Literacy: A National Program Helps Libraries Join Forces with Local Organizations to Boost Community Support," *American Libraries* 22 (March 1991): 256–58.

12. Susan Goldberg, "Community Action Now: Defying the Doomsayers," *Library Journal* 118 (March 15, 1993): 29.

13. http://www.urbanlibraries.org/about.html (accessed May 5, 2003).

14. Glen E. Holt, "Public Library Partnerships: Mission Driven Tools for 21st Century Success," 5, available at http://www.internationales-netzwerk.de/en/x_media/pdf/holt6en.pdf (accessed May 2, 2004).

15. Ibid., 35.

16. Norman Oder, "Three PLs Get Grants from IMLS," *Library Journal* 124 (October 15, 1999): 22.

2

The Williamsburg
Regional Library
Model for Partnering

Partnership development depends, to some extent, on the resources that the library has available to it, both internally and in the local community. However, all libraries have the opportunity to develop relationships with other community entities that support and enhance the mission of both groups. But where should a library's partnering effort begin? What are the best partnerships to develop within your community? How long will it take to develop a partnership program? Won't partnerships drain badly needed resources from an already overburdened library? These and other questions often are voiced when we begin to talk about embracing partnership development as a library strategy. In exploring ways that cross-sector partnering can be developed, it may be helpful to examine the background of the Williamsburg Regional Library system and the evolution of its partnership model.

Background of the Library and
Its Partnership Development Model

The Williamsburg (Virginia) Regional Library (WRL) could generally be categorized as a medium-sized public library. It consists of two buildings, the Williamsburg Library and the James City County Library, and a bookmobile, which serve a population of approximately 60,000. Approximately 80 percent of local residents have a library card. The library system is jointly funded by the city of Williamsburg and James City County, with a budget of $5,160,458 in FY05. The library is governed by a board of trustees, appointed by the city and the county. The Williamsburg Regional Library employs over 110 staff members, 70 full-time and 45 part-time. The library's collection exceeds 300,000 items, and the library circulates about one million items per year. The community is growing rapidly, and population projections predict a 20 percent increase between 2000 and 2010. The minority population is 17 percent according to the 2000 Census, down from 27 percent in 1970. The Williamsburg area is also a retirement destination,

11

and the over-sixty-five population is projected to increase to 17 percent by 2010. The mean household income for the area is $78,825, ninth highest in Virginia.

Like many libraries, Williamsburg Regional had worked over the years with outside organizations to put on programs or special events for library patrons. These efforts were usually made at the department level, with no librarywide coordination. In the spring of 1998, a representative of Sentara Williamsburg Community Hospital approached a librarian in the Adult Services Department with the question, "Would the library be interested in offering the community more cancer resources?" Although this was a seemingly simple question, it set in motion a series of events that would redirect how the library views its role in the community. Instead of simply seeing this question as a chance to expand the consumer health collection, the realization came that the library needed to take a new approach to serving the community, and that this approach involved developing formal partnerships with community organizations.

The hospital's interest in working with the library to provide cancer resources to the community had several results. The first was the development of the award-winning Phillip West Memorial Cancer Resource Center (CRC) (www.westcancer.org), one of the first cancer resource centers established in a public library. The CRC provides print, audiovisual, and electronic resources to cancer patients and their families, cancer survivors, the medical community and the general public, as well as a variety of educational programming throughout the year on cancer-related topics. The work on the development of this resource has led to the creation of a unique and ongoing partnership between the library and the hospital.

The development of these resources and programs could only have come about through the establishment of a long-term, committed relationship between the hospital and the library. This relationship became the model for future partnership development at WRL. It became clear that a partnership allowed the partners to combine resources and strengths to create new resources and services. To this particular project, the library brought its strengths in information organization, Web design, and providing assistance and instruction to the public in locating information. Other pluses were that the library was open seven days per week, and that it provided a less threatening environment for users than a medical establishment might. The hospital brought a strong public relations department, an understanding of the needs of local cancer patients, a connection to the medical community, and close ties to the local consumer health market. Putting these elements together has enabled the CRC to provide accurate and authoritative information on cancer throughout the community.

Another result of the hospital partnership was that library staff and administration came to understand the advantages of making partnership development a strategic direction for the library. It became clear that there were more partnering opportunities available in the community than the library had previously considered. Although the library had a sense of the value it could and did provide to individuals and the community as a whole, the hospital partnership brought to light the worth of WRL as an organization to other organizations. In a sense, partnering allowed WRL to become "the library" to local organizations, and a partnership agreement would formalize that relationship and bring WRL into the organization's structure.

The Williamsburg Regional Library Partnership Model

The Williamsburg Regional Library community partnership model is based on the following five principles:

1. The word "partnership" must be precisely defined by the library staff to make it useful and acceptable.

2. All sectors of the community—businesses, nonprofits, civic organizations, schools, governmental entities, and other libraries—are potential library partners.

3. Partnering serves a strategic purpose. It is one of several methods the library uses to implement the library's strategic plan.

4. Partnering is centrally coordinated and a formal process.

5. Partnership development is a librarywide strategy. All library staff and departments—including non-public service departments—and the library board of trustees have a unique role and responsibility to develop, support, and maintain the library's community partnerships.

Principle 1:
Define "Partnership" for Meaning in Your Library

A quick Google search of the Internet using the phrase "library partnerships" yields over 1,340,000 hits (March 2004). Probably each of these results is based on a different institutional definition of partnering. In many organizations, partnering is used to describe any type of outreach effort that involves working with another community group or organization. WRL has chosen to develop a layered definition of partnering, including the one-time programmatic events in which libraries have traditionally worked with outside organizations, but embracing a more intense, committed relationship model as well. For partnering efforts to work in any organization, there must be a clear understanding of what your institution defines as a partnership. An institutionally agreed upon definition is useful both within the organization as well as externally. Internally, a clear definition allows your library staff to see how partnering efforts fit in both the departmental and organizational work plans. Externally, the definition of partnering makes it clear to your potential partners what the library is trying to achieve through community partnership development. It is essential to establish clear definitions of what is and is not a partnership.

At WRL, the evolution of a tiered approach to defining partnering arose out of a librarywide discussion of how the library historically connected to the community and new methods of connecting as evidenced by the library's relationship with the Sentara Williamsburg Community Hospital. A committee was formed that included representatives from all library departments. The members of this committee ranged from circulation staff to the assistant library director. Including all levels of staff in the initial planning stages of partnership development proved a great tool for developing staff excitement about the process. One of the results of that process was the realization that while all partnerships between the library and community organizations are important, not all partnerships involve the same degree of institutional commitment or reward.

"Partnership" at WRL: A Definition That Works

To differentiate between the various degrees of community connections, WRL staff have identified the term "partnership" to include four types of community relationships: glances, dates, engagements, and marriages:

- **Glance:** Any overture or contact between the library and a community group, organization, business, school, or government agency. Glances may be in the form of written communications (including letters and e-mail); a visit; a telephone call; or participation in a group, club, or association as a library representative.

- **Date:** An agreement between the library and a community partner to accomplish a specific, short-term activity or commitment.

- **Engagement:** A formal agreement between the library and a community partner to work together toward a marriage after an experimental phase. Engagements are temporal: They either evolve into a marriage or dissolve.

- **Marriage:** A formal agreement between the library and a community partner with compatible goals, to share the work, the risk, and the results or proceeds. The library and the community partner jointly invest in resources; experience mutual benefits; and share risk, responsibility, authority, and accountability. Marriages form for long-term benefit to the partners.

The human relationship analogy has been successful for several reasons. It clearly lays out the levels of involvement in plain language, avoiding jargon that might be confusing to staff or outside organizations. Having a variety of levels also makes partnering more inclusive. All outside groups are recognized as offering value to the library, whether they are participating in a date or a marriage. At the same time, the efforts of all library staff are also recognized. Whether they are working on a large or a small project, staff partnering initiatives are included in the overall partnering concept. The relationship analogy also has an element of humor, which makes it more memorable. It is also expandable, and library staff have been heard talking about divorces, separations, trial marriages, marital counseling, and polygamy (partnerships with two similar organizations).

Outreach Versus Partnerships

As the WRL team clarified the definition of partnering, it quickly became evident that there is a clear distinction between "partnerships" and outreach programs. Under the WRL partnership model traditional library outreach activities are considered "library dates." "Dates" generally involve a one-time initiative, usually a program or event. Although these programs or events may have some support from an outside organization, the primary planning and execution are handled by library staff. The library provides a resource or program for a group. To effectively implement a formal partnering program, all staff at the organization should understand that "partnering" encompasses many levels of community relationships, including the traditional library outreach activities.

Library Promotion Versus Partnering

It is also important to distinguish between partnering efforts and library promotion. While marketing library services and resources may be part of a partnership, or even one of the main reasons for the establishment of a partnering relationship, partnering goes beyond simply bringing awareness of library resources and services to the community. Traditional promotional efforts are similar to traditional library outreach programs in that they are usually solo efforts by the library to promote resources or services. While the library may focus its promotion on a particular group or segment of the community, these efforts are generated by the library and sent out into the community. Although some promotion efforts may fall within the "date" category, most lack the multidimensional and collaborative features that distinguish partnership efforts.

Principle 2:
All Sectors of the Community Are Potential Partners

Library staff work with community organizations, businesses, civic groups, nonprofits, schools, libraries, and government entities to fulfill the library's mission of providing free access to information to all members of the community. Partnerships that are established must achieve at least one of the following goals to be considered successful:

- Reach new library users

- Reach current library users in a new way

- Tap into community assets and strengths

- Gain support for library resources and/or programs

- Gain valuable community feedback

- Create new resources

Few, if any, partnerships will achieve all of these objectives. When a formal engagement or marriage is being considered, it must have the possibility of meeting at least one of these goals.

Unlike most community organizations—nonprofits, businesses, educational institutions, even local governments—the public library serves the entire community. Especially in a regional system, the library is serving the needs of patrons across local government jurisdictions. This is one of the strengths that libraries bring to the table in partnership development; few, if any, other local groups serve as broad a population base as the library. At the same time, this raises challenges. With limited resources, in terms of both staff and funding, it can be very difficult for a library to reach out to every individual in the community.

Partnering approaches the situation from the opposite direction. Instead of working at the grassroots level, individual by individual, the library reaches out to the community through already existing organizations. By working in partnership with organizations that are "community gatekeepers," the library makes the best use of its resources and funds. Most community groups serve and market their resources to very specific groups. These can be church members, cancer patients, the elderly, etc. These groups focus their resources directly on these clients, and if they are successful, they build up a strong level of trust with their community. Working through established organizations allows the library to take advantage of the trust that the partnering group has built up within the community they serve. This can be a very effective method for the library to gain access to parts of its community where there may be some mistrust of the library or a lack of understanding about what the library has to offer. Working through a community partner enhances the presentation of resources to the community by working with this already established trust that the partner has built up and maintains.

Beyond the trust issue, there are several additional reasons for working through existing community groups in partnerships. By taking advantage of the partner's existing communication mechanisms the library can more easily and more effectively get its message out to the target group. In the case of the Phillip West Memorial Cancer Resource Center (CRC), the hospital already had in place an advertising and marketing system that could promote the center's resources and program. Promotion on this scale would have not been possible for the library to do alone, for both financial and staffing reasons.

Another value of working with established community partners is that they will bring a unique expertise in their specific area to the partnership. By combining this expertise with the library's strengths, the resulting partnership creates new resources and new services for users of both partnering organizations. The development of the CRC demonstrates how the marriage of strengths benefits not only both partners but also the community as a whole, which now has access to a broader and more complete selection of information and programming on cancer-related topics than was previously available.

While there are clearly advantages for the pubic library to operate in partnership with other community organizations, these organizations also need to be aware of the benefits that they will find in working with the public library. Organizations want to partner with the library for many of the same reasons that libraries want to partner with outside groups (see chapter 1 for a fuller discussion of the reasons that organizations partner with one another). They can take advantage of the library's unique strengths and skills to build new resources. By working in partnership, groups can work more efficiently, taking advantage of existing structures and mechanisms. Since, in most places, the library has a very high level of trust within the community, a group working as a library partner will be able to tap into that trust, in essence sharing the library's good name in the community. The breadth of the library's service area can dramatically expand the access of the partnering organization to different parts of the community. Many libraries can provide access to facilities, such as meeting rooms and program space, for the partner. Finally, the library can become the information-providing resource for the community partner.

Generally, partnerships form because there is some immediate situation that establishes a need or creates a project. In the case of the CRC, the Sentara Williamsburg Community Hospital was seeking national certification as a cancer treatment center, and the organization was required to provide access to cancer-related information to the community. At the same time, the hospital had received a bequest to assist in the expansion of the availability of cancer information in the community. Knowing that the public library had an active consumer health collection, hospital staff approached library staff about the possibility of expanding the cancer-related resources. This was the initial need that brought the two groups together. It resulted in the development of an award-winning cancer resource center and the commitment to an ongoing library/hospital marriage. Once the initial need is satisfied, both organizations must have some reason for the relationship to continue in order for the marriage to continue. In any partnership, the initial project becomes the mechanism through which trust is built between the partners. The development of a trust relationship allows the partnership to expand and take on new possibilities. How a library reaches out to all community sectors is explored in chapter 5.

Principle 3:
Partnering with Purpose

Prioritizing Partnerships

"If you don't know where you are going, you will probably end up somewhere else."[1]

Prioritization flows from the library's strategic plan. Setting priorities requires looking at where the partnership will take the library; if the organization does not know where it wants to go, as Peter and Hull point out, it will probably not get anywhere in particular. With a wealth of possible partnership opportunities, the need for some mechanism to set priorities becomes clear. For partnering to be successful, there must be an understanding of which community relationships can most benefit the organization. These are the partnerships that then can receive the most support in the form of resources and staff time.

There are numerous resources on developing strategic plans for all types of organizations, including libraries. A search for titles on strategic planning in libraries in OCLC's *First Search* database located over 375 monographs, including copies of strategic plans from a variety of libraries. A discussion of developing a strategic plan would require more space than is available here. However, there are some points that should be kept in mind when looking at planning and partnering.

The library's strategic plan flows out of the mission and vision that are established by the organization's governing body, the director, and the staff. Each of the departments in the library should be using this vision and direction in setting departmental work plans. These work plans must reflect the priorities of the librarywide plan. As each department is developing a work plan, potential areas for partnerships will become clear. These topical areas for partnerships—readers' advisory, consumer health, and service to young adults are some examples—all have possibilities to include partnering as a piece of the process. As the departmental work plans are being developed, partnering should be looked at as a potential tool to support the various projects and services offered.

There are two ways that departmental plans can incorporate partnering in their design. There are pros and cons to each method, and a balance of the two mechanisms may be the best way to achieve a consistent approach to partnering across departments and still get the support from all departments in the partnering process.

I. Each department takes the organization's strategic plan and designs its own partnering priorities based on that plan.

A. Pros

- Each department must assess its role in the library and be alert to what opportunities there are for innovation.
- Each department should have a better awareness of its own strengths and special talents.
- This approach is often seen as less threatening to departmental authority; rather than being dictated from above, the department sets its own priorities.
- Asking individual departments to share directly in partnership development should lead to a better understanding of the partnering process as well as increased willingness to participate in the process in the future.

B. Cons

- With each department setting its own partnering priorities, it can be difficult to bring all of these together to reflect librarywide priorities.
- The expression of partnering plans may not be as coherent across departments.
- Programs developed out of individual departments often tend to lean toward small initiatives, building incrementally on things that are already being done. It is easier to play it safe when developing plans than to exert the effort and take the risks that a librarywide partnership might involve.

II. A specially formed librarywide partnering team looks at the strategic plan and annually sets the priorities for the departments.

A. Pros

- A librarywide plan developed by a team composed of decision-making members of all library departments will be more coherent in scope and presentation.
- Cross-departmental communication in a team of this nature will encourage the development of larger and longer-term initiatives.
- The partnership development team model is likely to be more selective about what partnerships the library will take on.
- A dialog about partnering will be created at the management level of the library.

B. Cons

- Having a team present departments with projects that the department is expected to carry out can be seen as threatening to departmental autonomy.
- To get a buy-in from the departments, mechanisms need to be developed to involve frontline staff in the process (discussed in detail in chapter 4).

The Williamsburg Regional Library has found a combination of these two methods effective in prioritizing potential partnerships. Each department is encouraged to explore partnering possibilities as its annual work plan is developed. This allows the departments to assess their own abilities and establish directions. The partnership development group looks at these departmental plans and can suggest ideas for potential partnerships based on them. Any partnership plans that will develop into marriages with a community partner, as defined above, need to be brought to the partnership development group for discussion and approval prior to the development of a formal agreement with a potential partner.

Partnering Possibilities

With a mission statement, core values statement, and the library's strategic plan in hand, as well as a clear institutional definition of what is involved in the different levels of partnering, who are the groups that you partner with? Your community offers a variety of potential partners. The goals set in the library's planning process will help focus on the specific groups that you will want to consider as strategic partners. Clearly defining why the library partners and what the different levels of partnerships are allows the library to consider a broad range of potential partners. At the Williamsburg Regional Library, we have established seventeen marriages with organizations or businesses in the community. Using our definitions of partnering allows us to look at a broad range of potential partners, including

- nonprofit organizations,

- local schools (both public and private),

- government agencies,

- civic groups,

- businesses, and

- other libraries in the community.

All of these groups have assets that make them potential partners for the library, depending on the institution's mission and strategic plan.

Partnership Examples from the Williamsburg Regional Library

- Nonprofits

    - Sentara Williamsburg Community Hospital—This partnership supports the Phillip West Memorial Cancer Resource Center, bringing accurate and authoritative information to cancer patients and their families, survivors, caregivers, and the general public.

    - Williamsburg Community Health Foundation—The library and the foundation collaborate to build and promote the Funding Research Center, providing information on grants and grantwriting, and serving nonprofit organizations in the community.

- Local schools

    - Williamsburg-James City County Public Schools—As community partners the schools and library work together to (a) bring a love of reading and books to area students, (b) teach students to access and analyze information in all formats, and (c) support individuals in their goals for lifelong learning.

- Government agencies

    - James City County Neighborhood Connections—The library and Neighborhood Connections work together as community partners to achieve the following two goals: (a) to acquire new materials, catalog, circulate, and promote the Neighborhood Knowledge collection that is housed at the James City County Library (JCCL); and (b) to enhance the working relationship between the library and James City County by promoting the new collection and the partnership.

– Colonial National Historical Park—The partners work together to (a) promote the library as a place where patrons can learn about the local historical and natural environment; (b) promote Historic Jamestowne and Yorktown Battlefield as places to study and enjoy its history and natural resources; and (c) promote—by educating the public—the parks' historical significance. Through the partnership, the library and park have created new resources and seek to reach park and library users in new ways.

- Civic groups

  – League of Women Voters—The library and the League of Women Voters partner to offer the community information on public policy issues and to create a forum for citizen interaction and discussion.

- Businesses

  – Ukrop's—The community partners cooperate to (a) bring a love of reading and books to area children and their families, (b) conveniently serve library patrons and Ukrop's customers by providing selected off-site library services at the Ukrop's store, and (c) reach new users to the library by providing convenient, off-site access to selected library programs and services at the Ukrop's store.

- Other libraries

  – Swem Library at the College of William and Mary—The two libraries collaborate to plan, implement, and promote interlibrary initiatives to (a) increase the public, student, and faculty awareness of the resources at both libraries; (b) share resources and library programming; and (c) build staff development opportunities between institutions.

Nonprofits

Nonprofit groups are a good source for potential partnerships. Like libraries, nonprofits generally are set up to serve a specific community of users and often are directed in their missions to work collaboratively with other community organizations. From the library's perspective, a nonprofit group may be able to provide access to a unique group in the community that the library has historically had a difficult time reaching. The Sentara Williamsburg Community Hospital allowed the library to promote services and resources to a variety of nonprofit community health groups such as the Arthritis Foundation, the Williamsburg Alliance for the Mentally Ill, and the Alzheimer's Association. Another beneficial relationship for WRL has been a marriage with the Williamsburg Community Health Foundation. Although partnering with the nonprofit sector brings rewards, nonprofits also bring a particular set of challenges. They may be poorly funded, have small staff, and rely heavily on volunteers. All of these issues may be potential limitations to the relationship, and the stability of the organization should always be a consideration when deciding on a potential partner.

Schools

Local schools are also an obvious choice for potential partnerships. Particularly in the areas of literacy and information literacy, schools are interested in working together to share resources, and again can provide a good way for the library to reach a very broad group of potential users to promote resources and services. Initially our relationship with the local schools was on a school-by-school basis. However, a desire to clarify what the library is doing to support the schools and to reinforce the two-way nature of the relationship has led to the development of a formal agreement with the school system that outlines the role of each institution and the resources that each brings to the partnership.

Williamsburg Community Health Foundation Partnership

Williamsburg Community Health Foundation (WCHF), an area nonprofit organization, administers a community grant fund to support health-related community programs in the Williamsburg area. In 1999, the WCHF approached the Williamsburg Regional Library to discuss creating a grantsmanship resource center at the library. The foundation had been impressed by the library's successful partnership with the Sentara Williamsburg Community Hospital, which created the Phillip West Memorial Cancer Resource Center. Working together, the library and the foundation established the Funding Research Center in 2000.

The center, established with a $15,000 grant, assists area nonprofit organizations in their search for funding opportunities as well as providing "how to" information about developing and administering fund-raising programs. Through the partnership the library acquired over forty-five print resources for both the circulating and reference collections at the Williamsburg Library. The partners have also developed a Web page of more than 100 links to fund-raising and nonprofit organization related resources. The Funding Research Center Web address is http://www.wrl.org/depts/admin/frc.html.

The foundation continues to support the Funding Research Center materials, to cosponsor workshops and programs related to the center, and to explore new directions and opportunities for the partnership. In 2003, Adult Services staff from the library worked with the WCHF to beta-test an online community health atlas. Library staff are also helping to coordinate a series of workshops on legal and technology issues for nonprofit organizations in the community.

This partnership has allowed the library to develop an excellent relationship with a major foundation in the community. Working through a gatekeeper organization, the library has also been able to reach a new user group, area nonprofit organizations and individuals that are interested in grantwriting and fund-raising. It has also created a resource few public libraries of Williamsburg Regional Library's size can afford, and one that increases the library's visibility in the community. For more information on this partnership, see figure 6.3 (page 86).

Government

Working in partnership with government agencies, libraries can extend their reach into the community in new ways. In particular, working with local government agencies can help strengthen the understanding of the library by those responsible for its funding. A better appreciation of how the library operates in the community and of the value of the resources the library provides can be an asset at budget time. WRL has developed a partnership with a county agency to build and promote joint resources for neighborhood associations and homeowners' groups. Partnerships can also be established with state and federal agencies that operate in the community. The library has established partnerships with both state and national parks in the area to develop and share library and park resources with patrons.

Civic Groups

In trying to reach new users, or to gain support for library programs and services, civic group partnerships can be very valuable. Civic groups offer targeted populations to whom the library can promote its resources and services. Often, these populations may be groups that do not currently use the library. Reaching new users through a group that they already trust can be a good first step in letting them know that the library is also an organization that can be trusted.

Businesses

Partnerships with business can be among the most difficult to arrange but can also be fruitful for the library. As mentioned in chapter 1, the business sector was the first to realize the potential value of cross-sector partnering, and the pressures to partner in the private sector continue to be strong. There are concerns when developing long-term relationships with the for-profit sector. Among these is the difficulty of working with a for-profit organization that has competitors. The appearance that the library is favoring one business over others in the area is likely to occur in these situations. Problems can also arise when trying to match missions with for-profit organizations. Unlike libraries and other public sector organizations, a business organization's mission is usually directed toward profit. Partnerships with businesses require careful delineation of each partner's roles and responsibilities in the formal agreement, to ensure that the library does not simply become a mechanism for the business to realize its profit goals.

Libraries

It is probably easiest to establish a formal partnership with other libraries, since both institutions share a similar framework, mission, corporate culture, and language. Often these partnerships can build on already existing relationships, involving sharing resources, reaching out to similar audiences, etc. The Williamsburg Regional Library has a formal relationship with the Swem Library at the College of William and Mary dealing with such areas as interlibrary loan, joint staff development, promotion of resources, and programming.

Building on Trust

As mentioned previously, one of the reasons that a library will want to develop community partnerships is to reach out to potential new users through an organization that they already trust, building on the trust that the potential partner has already established with the people that it serves. Libraries, however, also have developed a substantial amount of trust in their communities throughout their existence. Even those in the community who do not use the library's resources on a consistent basis, if at all, often will say that they support the idea of the public library in the community. This trust is one of the library's greatest strengths when negotiating with potential partners, and it is essential that the library not squander that trust by developing poorly thought out or short-sighted partnerships.

Any time that the library participates in a joint venture, whether a one-time event or a long-term partnership, the trust that it has gained in the community is put at risk. Patrons are quick to sense when the relationship between the library and another community organization is one-sided or is not supportive of the library's mission. When working with outside organizations, libraries should avoid simply becoming part of that organization's marketing process. True partnering, like a true marriage, requires that both partners be clear about why they are getting involved in the relationship, and an understanding that the partners are working toward mutually agreed upon goals. Partnerships, like marriages, often break down when too much responsibility falls on one of the partners. Chapter 5 explores the process of examining the community for potential partnering opportunities and how to match the library's mission with that of possible partners.

Principle 4:
Partnering Is Centrally Coordinated and a Formal Process

Administration of Partnering Efforts

As the WRL team began to look at partnering as a strategy to fulfill its mission, it became evident that the organizational structure of the institution would have to change to more effectively pursue and implement community partnership development. First, there was a redefinition of the library's role within the community. While libraries have always done marketing and outreach to the community, these efforts have traditionally focused on what the library could do for individuals in the community. With the exception of regular bookmobile service, these efforts have tended to be one-time events or programs. Successful partnering requires a shift in perspective that encourages the library to look not only at how it serves individuals in the community but also at how it can serve those organizations in the community that have elements of their mission in common with the library. Rather than reaching out directly, person by person, now the library can reach individuals through some organization or group of which they are a part. This realization that partnering is a new means of reaching and serving individuals in the community is essential to a successful partnership program.

Staffing a Partnership Program

The library also found it necessary to develop an administrative position to coordinate community partnership development on a librarywide scale. At WRL, the position of community partnership development director was established to oversee and direct the development of partnerships from the initial exploration through establishment to evaluation. The partnership director position has a role similar to that of a marketing or development coordinator, focusing on the library's partnering strategy. Having a position dedicated to partnership development also gives credibility to the library's efforts within the community.

Having a partnership director helps to create a librarywide understanding of the goals and mechanisms of partnering. Partnerships can be developed at any level of the organization, and for the concept of partnering to be understood and to thrive, all staff should feel encouraged to participate in partnership development. However, if partnering is to be an institutional tool for achieving the organization's mission, central coordination is essential. The partnership director is a specialist, looking at the library and the community and seeing those opportunities for the two to intersect in a way that supports the library's mission and its strategic plan.

Because the position is located in administration, as a development or marketing position would be, the partnership director should be viewed as a neutral figure, without a perceived departmental bias. Since partnerships inevitably cross departmental lines in terms of management roles and responsibilities, having a position that can look beyond the confines of a departmental work plan and see how the partnership may affect the work of other library areas is important to the success of the partnering strategy. In some institutions, it may be difficult to develop interdepartmental cooperation on large-scale projects. Department heads might be reluctant to give up control of their staff resources and time or to look beyond departmental priorities. Interdepartmental projects can be seen as a threat to departmental autonomy. Without central coordination, it is possible that an important partnering opportunity could be missed because of poor interdepartmental cooperation. A partnership director can forestall these problems by ensuring that ideas are not tied up by department politics. The role of the community partnership development director will be more fully explored in chapter 4.

Principle 5:
Partnership Development Is a Librarywide Strategy

Cross-Departmental Nature of Partnership Development

A successful library partnership program will bring benefits to the library beyond the development of new resources and services. As mentioned previously, most partnerships that develop between the library and community organizations involve the efforts of more than a single library department. Some partnerships at WRL have involved staff from as many as four different departments. For partnerships to succeed in this collaborative environment, communication between departments must be strong. The development of an active partnership program requires departments to interact more directly to avoid misunderstandings, ultimately increasing communication pathways throughout the organization.

Allowing staff from a variety of departments to work together on partnership projects strengthens the identity of the organization. Staff members feel committed to the success of the library, not only to the success of their department. Library staff members can also develop a better sense of what each department does to support the organization's mission. In addition to improving communication between departments, this understanding also fosters a sense of the importance of looking at the library as a whole, rather than as separate units, "guarded by" department heads.

Another benefit that the cross-departmental nature of partnerships brings to the library is the increased interaction between public service and support service departments. Too often in libraries the support departments—technical services, automated services, etc.—are marginalized by the public service departments. Partnering efforts require staff from all of the library's departments to work collaboratively. In this environment, it is easier to recognize that the work of all library departments is essential and interrelated, and that the work of all staff members contributes to the success of the organization.

Increased interdepartmental cooperation also leads to increased departmental buy-in to the partnering process. If a department feels that the time and staff resources that they contribute to a partnership are recognized, they are more likely to want to participate in the process. In addition, staff from various departments have the opportunity to clearly discuss how a proposed partnership will affect their operations. This, in turn, makes it easier for the organization to prioritize partnering efforts. It is difficult to make decisions about the relative value and merits of partnering opportunities without a clear understanding of the impact that they will have on library operations at all levels. Increased collaboration between departments will result in a better understanding of what is required by a particular partnership.

Additional dimensions of the impact of partnering strategies on library staff are explored in chapters 4 and 8.

Note

1. Laurence J. Peter and Raymond Hull, *The Peter Principle,* quoted in *The New York Public Library Book of 20th-Century American Quotations,* ed. Stephen Donadio et al., 68 (New York: Warner Books, 1992).

3

Internal Foundations for Partnership Development

Although relationships with outside organizations can be formed at any time, an internal foundation needs to be established within the library to give purpose, direction, and coherence to the process. Taking the following steps will allow the library to have a coherent, organizationwide approach to partnership development:

- Create a strategic plan for the institution that includes partnering as both a strategic direction and a primary focus for the library.

- Assess and make a list of assets and strengths that the library offers as a community partner.

- Establish an internal mechanism for communication related to partnering for decision-making, management, and idea generation.

- Build a partnering program plan that sets out librarywide partnership development policies, as well as processes for management of partnerships.

Step One: Create a Strategic Plan

As mentioned in chapter 2, the impetus for partnering must flow from the organization's strategic plan. The inclusion of partnering as a tool to achieve the goals of the organization reinforces, both internally and externally, the value that is placed on partnership development. The creation or refinement of a strategic plan provides several opportunities to promote the concept of partnering in the library. This will be beneficial in the long run, as staff support of the concept is necessary for its success. Emphasis on partnering as a tool for achieving institutional goals also indicates the value placed on partnering by the administration. Library staff understand that time spent on partnership development is a priority for the library. Library boards and funding bodies understand why the organization is spending resources on partnership development. Potential partners are alerted that the organization is seeking out new relationships in the community.

The strategic plan can also generate excitement within the institution and the community about what the future holds. From the perspective of partnership development, this excitement can build much-needed support for partnering. For this reason, it is to the advantage of the institution to make the development of this plan as open a process as possible. By including many different points of view in the development of the institution's plan, key players in supporting the organization will be brought on board, and partnering will be brought to the forefront.

- **Library staff input:** In the planning process, library staff from all departments and all levels of the organization should be involved in as many ways as possible. Gathering input from staff through surveys, focus groups, and staff planning committees will enhance the staff buy-in on the finished product. This is particularly important from the partnership development perspective, as partnering flourishes when all staff can participate in the process.

- **Community input:** Focus groups, surveys, town hall meetings, and other tools allow the public to have input into the organization's planning process. It is also important to involve in the process not only individual members of the public but also representatives of those organizations that are community gatekeepers. These are the organizations that the library will want to work with as community partners, and allowing them to feel that they have a stake in planning where the library is headed creates fertile ground for future relationships.

Having a strategic plan implies that the library is positioning itself to achieve specific goals within a set period of time. The mission statement, vision, and strategic directions sections of a strategic plan are the most important sections in driving partnership development within the institution. A mission statement expresses the values of an institution, and in exploring potential partnerships, it is essential that the two partners have harmonious missions. A careful examination of a prospective partner's mission statement will help determine if the partner can work in a committed way with the library. The mission statements of both partners should express ideas that cement the organizations' shared values and purposes. We examine how to match mission statements further in chapter 5. The vision statements set out specific goals for the institution and should also set out a time frame for achieving these goals. See the example in the box.

VISION

In 2005, the residents of Williamsburg, James City County, and Upper York County will recognize that the Williamsburg Regional Library:

- Is the first source for community information needs and a welcoming presence for new arrivals, helping them connect with the community.

- Provides a friendly and informed staff who are vital parts of the cultural, social, and educational life of the community.

- Has a dynamic collection of materials that is regularly evaluated and available in a variety of formats to serve the needs and support the interests of all members of our community.

- Seeks the most appropriate technological innovations while maintaining a strong commitment to traditional library services.

- Extends services beyond its walls, seeking out increasing access points for information, collections, and programs.

- Provides early language experiences for all children in the community.

- Teaches community members how to gather, evaluate, and use information.

- Creates partnerships with civic organizations, educational and government entities, businesses, and libraries to reach new user groups and expand access to library services.

- Is a community center that encourages and supports interaction among all our residents.

- Is a responsible steward of its available resources.

Based on these goals, the institution looks for partnership opportunities that will help to meet these goals. Similarly, the goals are used to evaluate and prioritize potential partnerships.

Step Two: Assessing Assets and Strengths

Some institutions may be reluctant to make the time commitment necessary to develop a strategic plan prior to implementing partnership development in their institution. We consider this to be a mistake, because without a strategic plan, or at the very least individual department plans, the library has no clearly defined reason to implement partnering. The strategic plan defines the core values of the institution and gives direction to staff in developing partnerships. If, however, library management does not feel capable of developing a complete strategic plan, there are some planning functions directly necessary to partnership development that should be carried out prior to looking for partnering opportunities. One is the crafting of a mission statement that, as described above, identifies the library's values. However, the task that is most practical to partnering is the development of a list of the assets and strengths of the library.

To most effectively present the institution to potential partners, it is essential that there be a shared sense of what the library has to offer those partners. What sort of resources does the library have that are unique to the community, that are of value, and that are marketable? These assets and strengths are what will attract potential partners to the organization and will be effective bargaining tools when cementing a partnership agreement.

Institutional assets and strengths fall into two broad categories, tangible and intangible. Each is important to the partnering process, and it is important to draw out examples of each of these strengths when developing the list. Following are some examples of tangible and intangible assets that a library might consider in developing its list:

- **Tangible assets**

    - Library meeting rooms

    - Library collections (in multiple formats)

    - Public computers

    - Computer labs

    - Special services for the disabled (low-vision computers, hearing-assisted meeting rooms, etc.)

    - Library hours

- **Intangible strengths**

    – Library staff expertise

    – Understanding of the broad information landscape

    – Community trust

    – Library serves all markets and ages in the community

    – Public service emphasis

    – Interdepartmental cooperation

The most effective means for determining the institution's assets and strengths is to involve all the staff in creating a list of these resources. This can be done in a variety of ways but is most effective when done as part of an organizationwide meeting. Creating an assets and strengths list with all staff present allows staff from different departments interact with each other rather than focusing on single departments' perspectives. Following are the steps for making the most of the process at a general staff meeting:

1. Break the larger group into several smaller groups, five to eight people per group. Make sure that each group contains staff members from various departments or sections of the organization. Mix together public service staff, administrative staff, and staff who work only behind the scenes.

2. Each smaller group should have a facilitator who has been prepared in advance to be able to keep the discussion flowing. The facilitator can have a list of types of assets and strengths similar to those mentioned above to use as examples if the discussion slows down. The facilitator should also be prepared to keep the focus centered on creating the list.

3. Give the groups fifteen to twenty minutes to brainstorm items for the assets and strengths list, encouraging each group to think as broadly about the library as possible.

4. Bring the small teams back to report out to the larger group. The reporting out period allows for further expansion of the list of assets and strengths as ideas reported generate new ideas among the staff. In addition, reporting out reinforces commonly held ideas. When staff realize that many of the assets and strengths they came up with are similar to those the other groups thought of, it reinforces or validates that they have a good understanding of the institution.

5. When the ideas have all been collected, a document should be developed that lists all of the perceived assets and strengths. This can then be circulated among staff for further comment and additions. This document will be of great use to staff as they explore potential partnering opportunities. Knowledge of what the library has to offer as a partner is an invaluable tool to attract community organizations. When floating an idea with a potential community partner, understanding of the value the library brings to the relationship allows the library staff person to make a stronger presentation. At the same time, an understanding of the library's assets and strengths will make it easier to clarify to a potential partner what the library cannot do in a relationship.

The creation of the assets and strengths list has direct application in partnership development. At the very basic level, a clear assessment of what the library has to offer will determine whether the organization can actually engage in the partnering process. If, after creating the list, the tally of assets and strengths is small, it may not be practical for the library to plan on developing partnerships initially. The list will point out the institution's limitations and offer two possibilities.

First, the organization may decide not to engage in certain types of partnering projects because it does not have the resources to offer. Conversely, the organization can look at the limitations as outlined in the assets and strengths list and see where resources need to be added, using the list as a tool to build up the library's assets to the point at which partnering becomes a viable possibility.

To successfully develop a partnering program, the library must have resources to offer to a potential partner. The development of the assets and strengths list will clearly define what these resources are and allow the library to negotiate with outside organizations. Figure 3.1 is the assets and strengths list developed by staff at the Williamsburg Regional Library.

Figure 3.1. Assets and Strengths

Williamsburg Regional Library Assets and Strengths

Williamsburg Regional Library combines assets and strengths to offer the community valuable resources and programs. When developing a community partnership it is important to know what the library has to offer a given area organization or business that is unique, valuable, and marketable. These assets and strengths are what attract a potential partner to the library and are effective bargaining tools when negotiating a partnership agreement. The following list of the library's assets and strengths was created by the staff.

ASSETS

Facilities

- two library locations + bookmobile
- aesthetically pleasing buildings
- beautiful landscape (including sculptures)
- 6 total meeting room spaces at both buildings (accommodates a variety of group sizes and needs)
- 268 capacity theatre
- eCLIC room—computer lab (8 computer/printer stations)
- art exhibit space—gallery
- quiet study rooms at both buildings
- story garden at James City County Library
- adequate parking
- public restrooms
- air conditioned buildings
- comfortable seating
- display space
- public notice boards and handout racks at both buildings
- classroom space
- hearing impaired equipped meeting rooms
- meeting rooms in each facility with attached kitchens
- close proximity to restaurants and shopping (Williamsburg Library)
- theatre is a top rated venue for musical performers

Figure 3.1. (*Cont.*)

Equipment

- public computer stations with Internet and software—word processing, spreadsheets, and Power Point
- public copy machines
- low vision computers with large font (24)
- public typewriters
- network printers
- smart board (eCLIC room)
- wireless network
- sound system
- light system
- color copier in Youth Services Department
- scanners
- new overhead LCD projector in James City County Library Community Room
- remote access
- motorized cart for the disabled at James City County Library
- shopping cart for patron use at James City County Library
- microfiche, microfilm and reader printers
- Automatic External Defibrilators (AEDs)
- development software
- partnership database
- shuttle van running between buildings
- back-up van
- performance piano
- PC Reliance—remote check out system
- CPR manikins
- LCD projectors at both buildings
- Hearing assist systems at the Williamsburg Library Theatre and James City County Library Community Room

Collection

- reference collection
- strong consumer health collection
- Large Print collection
- Phillip West Memorial Cancer Resource Center
- large, extensive, current collection in a variety of media including 297,416 books, 4,672 CDs, 17,956 videos, 2,440 DVDs, 410 magazine subscriptions + newspapers and 12,108 audiotapes
- Genealogy Resource Center
- fiction collection that includes new authors
- African American fiction
- WRL website

Continued →

Figure 3.1. (*Cont.*)

- Lit Kits
- Junior Lit Kits
- Park Packs
- Gab Bags for book discussion groups
- Matthew Whaley Resource Center
- educational toys in Youth Services Department
- electronic resources
- home access to magazine databases
- business resources
- Bi-Folkal Kits
- bilingual materials
- parents corner collection
- Funding Research Center
- topical research guides to the collection
- James City County—Neighborhood Knowledge collection
- fiction guides by interest
- fiction bookmarks—read-alike lists
- classic movie selection
- foreign film videos
- children's videos
- non-feature video collection
- Learn a Test database—GED, ASVAB
- Local Authors collection
- Local Organizations directory

STRENGTHS

Services

- open 7 days a week
- morning and evening hours
- patron reserves—online and on-site
- free, unfiltered Internet use
- filtered Internet option in Youth Services department
- beverages allowed policy
- Interlibrary Loan
- generous library card privileges—40-item limit
- library cards to anyone, anywhere in Virginia with the proper identification
- tourist cards
- teacher cards
- numerous community outreach activities—all departments
- online renewal of materials

Continued →

Figure 3.1. (*Cont.*)

- TeleCirc—electronic notification and renewal system via telephone
- book donation pick-up service
- old books and magazines accepted by Friends of the Library
- proctor exams
- reference service
- gifts and memorial opportunities
- circulating children's magazines
- external book drop
- off site book drop at Ukrop's
- volunteer computer assistance
- no shelving back log
- quick ordering, cataloging, processing
- few fee based services (copiers, printers)
- tax forms, AARP Tax Aide program
- free notary service
- list servs (Beacon of Freedom Award, WRL-Info)
- monthly library newsletter
- receptionists
- electronic weekly newsletter and events calendar
- electronic book discussion—Read/Write
- teaches children literacy skills
- public suggestion box
- book displays
- Ask a Librarian email reference
- Friends of Library sale on site at both buildings
- outreach to book discussion groups
- Homebound program delivery service
- Web based patron access catalog
- respite care
- browser's copies of books
- electronic calendar of events
- WRL book Web
- Web links selected by Adult Services librarians
- recommend books to read
- help students find information
- teaches research skills, use of computer reference sources

Programs

- AARP Tax Aide
- book discussion groups—adults and youth
- story times
- cancer related education programs

Continued →

Figure 3.1. (*Cont.*)

- Dewey Decibel concert series
- Battle of the Books
- home school audience programs
- Internet classes
- Summer Reading
- teen programs
    - summer volunteers
    - Treats for Teens
    - Reading Rampage
- Bookmobile Programs
- Feed Me a Story story time held at Ukrop's Grocery Store each Saturday
- Mother Goose Programs
- community events (Dog Days, Bad Poetry, Library Fest etc.)
- Mother Read/Father Read program
- B.A.B.Y program
- partnership program
- Adult Basic Education/English as a Second Language classes
- League of Women Voters
- Great Decisions series
- Williamsburg Area Learning Tree partnership classes
- Living Well on the Web Internet classes
- Beacon of Freedom Award
- Classics in the Library theatre productions
- Croaker Cabaret
- Lit-Flick book/film discussion
- author visits
- poets forum
- Saturday poetry series
- concerts
- exhibits and displays
- live theatre
- Celtic film series
- school group tours of the library
- Music In Your Life series (with the Friends of the Virginia Symphony)
- Spanish classes (occasional)
- Local Author series
- Paws at your Library

Staff

- well trained, knowledgeable staff
- creative and enthusiastic staff
- Adult Services librarians have Master's Degrees in library science

Continued →

Figure 3.1. (*Cont.*)

- dedicated to customer service—willingness to go the extra mile
- awareness of outside libraries' resources
- experience organizing and accessing information
- variety of talents of staff
- consistently strive to improve and excel
- flexibility and responsiveness
- efficient use of resources
- staff comfortable with change
- excellent departmental leadership
- fiscally responsible and effective staff—thrifty spenders of library funding
- staff cross-training between departments
- aware of what public wants and needs
- staff with a sense of humor
- volunteers
- off site computer technician
- Program Services technicians
- Staff Development Committee
- broad staff involvement in the community
- inter-departmental cooperation
- graphic designer
- Automated Services staff expertise

Miscellaneous

- community support
- positive and trusted image in community
- high visibility in community
- local funding
- Friends of WRL
- strong public school/library relationship
- WRL Foundation
- supportive Board of Trustees
- embrace technology
- given the freedom to innovate (fail)
- openness to public requests
- successful community partnerships as models
- responsive to public concerns
- high per capita funding
- promotional ability
- accessibility—community integration
- friendly work environment
- location of buildings
- local, state, and national reputation

Continued →

Figure 3.1. (*Cont.*)

- serve an entire spectrum of ages, religions, and economic levels
- multiplicity of services and methods
- diverse constituents
- flexibility of scheduling for staff
- strong stance on intellectual freedom
- sophisticated patrons
- link to homeschool community
- building on existing community links
- give value back to the community
- Strategic Plan
- flexibility as a large organization, able to take quick action
- focused as a group
- library is recognized as an information center and an entertainment center
- can use technology to market library resources
- relationship with James City County
- technologically mobile
- advocacy for children
- Community partnership program
- Development office
- successfully awarded grants
- annual audit
- Support Services department—quickly processes new and added materials
- regularly weeded collections

One resource that almost all libraries can count on is a sense of trust from their communities. Historically, libraries have been perceived by the public as valued institutions, and over the past two centuries they have built up a very positive image in the community. However, this trust alone is not enough of a basis on which to establish partnerships. Partnerships require a significant investment of time to establish. To justify the use of library staff time and resources the organization must have a meaningful return from the community partner. If the library only has its good name in the community to offer as a bargaining piece, it probably will not be able to negotiate a substantive exchange with a partner.

The library's partnership managers will be able to use the assets and strengths list as a tool for partnership development. It enables partnership managers to consistently present what the library has to offer as an institution. The list makes the managers aware of the possibilities and limitations of what the library can do and offer.

In addition to providing a foundation for working with potential partners, the development of an assets and strengths list brings added value to the library. Although these additional benefits will be valuable to the partnering effort, they extend beyond partnering and will strengthen the organization as a whole:

- Involving the entire organization in preparing the list brings staff together in a new way and encourages thinking across departmental lines. Increased cross-departmental participation in library projects and services will benefit both the institution and its patrons by increasing efficiency through cooperation. As an added benefit, this sort of cross-departmental cooperation tends to break down isolation and builds a sense of cohesiveness within the organization.

- By taking a broad view of the library during the process, the creation of the assets and strengths list increases staff insight into the interrelated nature of the organization. This understanding is essential to successful partnering. As individuals in the library seek out and develop partnerships, they need to be aware of how the potential partnership will affect all areas in the organization. Although the partnership may seem to be a simple one, there are often implications for the entire institution that will be easier to identify if staff understand how the organization operates as a whole.

- When done in an institutionwide fashion, the development of the assets and strengths list will increase the sense of staff ownership in the process. This is important for partnership development in the institution, as will be seen in later chapters that discuss how partnering can and should arise for all levels of the organization.

- The assets and strengths list is a useful tool in promoting the library to the library board, to funding bodies, and to new or potential staff. It clearly lays out what makes the library a strong and valuable entity in the community. It also can be a useful tool in justifying funding levels or in seeking additional funding.

Step Three: Documenting and Tracking Partnering

One of the most important elements in developing the internal foundation for partnership development in the library is establishing a mechanism to track the library's collaborative efforts. There are myriad ways to document partnering efforts, everything from paper files to electronic databases. Regardless of what method you choose, tracking partnership development will be an asset to your endeavor.

What do you want to track? We believe that for the library to have the best understanding of the various connections in the community it is important to try to track *all* interactions between library staff and outside organizations. Using the courtship analogy, this would mean that you are tracking not only marriages but also dates and engagement, and even glances. Although it is more time-consuming to document these less formal community contacts, in the long run your library will benefit. Tracking contacts allows the library to develop a more comprehensive picture of who it is working with in the community and what the possibilities are for developing new partnerships.

A tracking mechanism documents what is going on in the library regarding partnering. By having a shared and open record of contacts and discussions with the various groups in the community, the library can avoid the embarrassment of different staff or departments unknowingly talking to the same organization. The partnering effort looks less than professional when a prospective partner says, "You are the third person from your organization to talk to us about this, don't you all communicate?" Whatever sort of tracking mechanisms are used, the goal should be to create a clearinghouse of information on ways the library interfaces with the community.

An information clearinghouse also avoids confusion within the library by clarifying who on staff may be working with what organizations in the community. Knowing who at the library has already spoken with a particular organization also can help you evaluate the partnership potential of that organization. If a library staff person has found a particular organization difficult to work with, that information will be useful when considering a partnership with that group.

Another reason for setting up a formal tracking mechanism for partnerships is to clarify for a potential partner all of the things that the library is already doing to support that particular institution. There may be institutions in the community with which the library already has a strong connection. This relationship may involve programming, services, resources, or other functions. Sometimes these relationships that began as small interactions have grown over time into projects that require significant investment of resources.

Other relationships may be very one-sided, with the library giving and the community institution taking. In many cases, several library departments may be working on various projects with an individual institution. Unless there is a strong mechanism for communicating these sorts of projects within the library, it is easy to look at each project individually, rather than seeing that library resources (staff, time, perhaps even money) are going to work with a single institution. Having a tracking mechanism makes it easy to see the bigger picture.

As an example, the Williamsburg Regional Library has for many years worked on various projects with local public schools. Initiatives were developed and carried out by library staff in all public service departments. When we started tracking contacts in the community, it quickly became clear that because of the large amount of support we were already giving the schools, that there was an opportunity to build a formal partnering relationship. Having a clear picture of what we were already doing on a school-by-school basis made it easier for the library to pitch a partnership to the school system. We were able to demonstrate how by developing a formal partnering relationship we could improve on our already existing association. A formal relationship would allow us to clarify initiatives and to offer a more consistent package of opportunities to the entire school system. Our presentation was successful, and we now have a flourishing partnership with the local school system that increases our access to a broad spectrum of the community.

Another reason for tracking community contacts in support of partnering efforts is that it documents the partnering process over time. Having information on community contacts and what the library has done in the past with these organizations is a way of building in institutional memory. There is less of a concern about the effect of staff turnover on already existing relationships if new staff members know where to look to find out what has happened in the past.

Mechanisms for Tracking Partnering

Williamsburg Regional Library has found that tracking and documenting partnering efforts is facilitated by the use of technology. We use both database management software and the Internet to help us follow relationships and to share information both internally and with partners. While there will be some costs involved in building a database of partnering activities, we feel that the financial and staff time expenses are justified by the ease with which information can be stored and retrieved with these systems.

There are several pieces of information that are useful to collect in the partnership database. Using whatever software your library has chosen, set up data fields for the following:

- Organization name

- Organization type (business, civic, government, school, nonprofit, library)

- Contact person at that organization

- Level of commitment (glance, date, engagement, or marriage)

- Library staff contact(s)

- Date of the contact

- Time commitment of relationship (if there is one)

- Brief description of the relationship or contact

- Name of person creating the record

- Link to letter of agreement (if one exists)

When you are designing the structure of the database, it is important to keep in mind how you plan to use the information it contains. It is a good idea for the staff who will be using the database to participate in its design to ensure that it will meet the library's needs for reporting and tracking partnerships. There are several points to consider when putting the database structure together:

- What information is important to the library? We have found that the basic information detailed above allows us to get a good sense of the community and of potential partners when we look at the data. However, each library's situation is different, and it is important to remember that this database is an internal tool that will be used by library staff. As with the development of any cross-departmental tool, it is essential to get comments on the structure from all parts of the organization.

- Don't overwhelm staff. As you develop the database, be sure not to include so much information that it becomes difficult or time-consuming for staff to enter information. If staff feel that entering information on community contact is onerous, they will simply not do it, and the resulting database will not give a useful portrait of the community and of potential partners therein. Entering items in the database should be made as simple as possible.

- Entries should be able to be linked together. As noted above, the information in the database need not be exhaustive. Pick the most essential information to include in the database. Remember that the database is supposed to allow staff to see at a glance who may have already talked to someone in a particular organization, and too much information will slow down this process.

Once the database is constructed, all staff members should be encouraged to enter information there on community contacts. In addition to listing formal partnerships (engagements and marriages), the database should also be used to track dates and glances. By including all levels of relationships in the database, you can more easily coordinate efforts, rather than spending time finding out whether the library has worked with a potential community partner in the past.

We have chosen to limit access to the partnership database solely to library staff. There seems to be no need to allow community partners, actual or potential, to view this information or to create entries. The database is solely for the library to use in tracking and coordinating relationships internally. Within the library, all staff should have access to the partnership database.

There is also partnership information that will be of interest to community partners. In addition to using the partnership database to track community relationships and provide information on partnering to library staff, we have found it very useful to set up a partnership development Web site that can be accessed by both library staff and community partners. The content and design of the partnership Web site was developed by those members of the library staff who are partnership managers. The primary purpose of the Web site is to provide information on the mechanics of partnering, and it was most logical that the partnership managers would best know what information they need to be effective. Sample pages from the partnership Web site are include in chapter 8.

The information on the Web site is aimed at four audiences: (1) library staff and board members, (2) specific partnership managers, (3) the library's partnership administrative group, and (4) community partners (both existing and potential). As we mentioned in discussing the partnership database, the information included on the partnership Web site should be tailored to the specific needs of the library's partnering program. What follows is a discussion of those elements on the Web site that we have found to be most useful for developing partnerships.

Library Staff and Board Members

The section of the partnership site that is addressed to library staff in general is intended to define and explain what the partnership development program at the library does and why it is important. On the staff part of the site, we have included the following information:

- Information on current partnerships (a brief list of engagements and marriages, including the library partnership manager and a short summary of the major initiatives) and links to letters of agreement for all marriages

- Links to all of the partnership forms (proposal form, partnership evaluation form, and program evaluation form)

- Information pages on initiating and managing a partnership (in both step-wise and flow chart form)

- The goals and definitions of partnering at the library

- An outline and description of the roles of those involved in partnering (staff, partnership development director, department heads, library director, and library board)

- List of assets and strengths of the library

- Links to the library's strategic plan and mission statement

Partnership Managers

The partnership managers' section of the site includes all of the information that is available to general library staff. In addition, this section contains the tools that the partnership managers need to create and manage partnerships in a uniform way. Having all of this information available to current and potential partnership managers via the Internet helps to ensure consistency in the process of developing relationships with community groups. The following are included in the managers' section:

- all of the information for staff listed above, plus

- a frequently asked questions section that covers information on the library and the partnering process, and

- standards for publicizing partnership events.

Partnership Development Group

In addition to sections for staff and partnership managers, we set aside a portion of the library's partnership Web site for information about the partnership development group. The role of this group in partnership development is more fully explored in chapter 4, but the group's primary charge is to "facilitate a strategic and integrated approach to partnering" within the library.

The group is made up of the heads of all the library's public service departments as well as the assistant director, the development director, and the partnership development director. Information on this section of the site is provided both for the use of this group and for all staff to review. As a communication piece, this section of the site creates a level of transparency on the process of partnership development in the library. Staff can look at meeting minutes and the archives of the group's e-mail list and can get a better sense of where partnering is going. This section also includes internal documents that the group uses in considering new partnership proposals. The partnership group section of the site contains the following:

- The group's charge

- A list of members

- Meeting minutes

- Mailing list archive

- Proposal review questions

Existing and Prospective Partners

Having the information about the library's partnering program available for potential partners via the Internet has a number of advantages. It is an excellent way of communicating the program to prospective partners and answering some of their questions more quickly. It also serves as a means to communicate the seriousness of the process to prospective partners. The terms "partnership" and "partner" have been so overused that few people have a clear idea of what they mean within a particular context. The information that you include here allows you to convey what your particular institution means by those terms. Making clear the definitions and expectations of a partnering program this way can also deter potential partners who are not willing to commit the time and energy to develop a mutually beneficial relationship. Those organizations that are simply looking for the library to give them something in return for little or nothing will be surprised to discover what the library expects of its partners, both in time and in resources.

The partners' section of the Web site includes information on specifics and procedures of partnering that will be useful for the partner. This is a useful place to share any deadlines for publicity that the partner should know, as well as other information of this sort. There are several other topics covered here:

- Definition of partnering

- Goals

- Current partnerships information

- Frequently asked questions

- Forms

- Publicity

- Community partnership development group charge

- Links to the library's mission statement and strategic plan

Developing a comprehensive resource of partnering information and sharing that information among library staff and community partners (current and potential) will strengthen the overall partnership program at the library. Among staff, the Web site serves to improve communication, increase transparency of the process, build excitement among staff, and act as a training tool for new partnership managers. In working with community partners, the Web site can become a tool for selling the idea of partnering, a means to emphasize that the library takes partnering seriously, a way of conveying expectations to existing and prospective partners, and a mechanism to communicate procedures.

Regardless of the methods and technology used, the more information the library can gather on its interactions with community organizations, the more successful the partnership program will be. These records can be used to communicate partnering goals and procedures to both library staff and community partners. Making partnership documents easily available to all library staff encourages active participation in the partnering process. Keeping partnering activities visible to both library staff and to the community increases both understanding of and excitement about the value of developing strong relationships within the community.

This chapter covers the first three steps in creating a structure that will support partnership development in your library. The next chapter looks at the fourth step: setting up librarywide policies and procedures that support and promote partnership development.

4

Setting up the Internal Structure for Partnering

Once the basic foundations for partnering have been established—a well-crafted strategic plan, an understanding of the assets and strengths the library offers, and a mechanism for tracking partnership development—the next issue to be addressed is how to ensure that the internal structure of the library supports and encourages partnership development. Although it is possible, and possibly tempting, to simply head into partnership building without looking at the library's internal structure, doing so would force you to pass up valuable opportunities that arise in the process and would weaken your endeavor.

There are three integral reasons for having or developing an administrative framework for partnership development:

1. To generate ideas and ensure that they are carried out

    a. A formal structure says to staff that partnering is an important tool for carrying out the library's vision and mission.

    b. It also establishes a mechanism to ensure that good ideas do not disappear simply because of departmental disinterest.

2. To coordinate the development of partnerships librarywide and to set priorities for partnering within the library

3. To manage individual partnerships

When considering initiating a partnering program at the library, it is easy to think that existing administrative structures will be able to handle these operations. Setting up new structures is a time-consuming process and may involve shifting priorities within the institution and restructuring communication channels. None of these aspects appeal to library staff who already feel that they have too much to do and not enough time to do it. Nonetheless, we recommend at least considering how your existing structures must be modified to better support partnership development. Here's why.

First, partnering requires that library departments work together cooperatively, not just on specific projects, but in developing long-term goals and priorities. While interdepartmental cooperation is common in libraries already, active partnership development demands a willingness on the part of all departments to share not only resources and time but also some departmental autonomy. Partnering will not be successful if each department jealously guards its community contacts and programs. In some libraries, there may already exist a climate of strong interdepartmental decision making. These fortunate institutions may not need to develop a new administrative structure for partnership development. Most institutions, however, will find that a new structure facilitates the promotion of this sort of cross-department cooperation.

Second, partnership development will only thrive if there is someone in the library who is taking an institutionwide view of the process. Although the hope is that all library staff will begin to look at planning and projects in a broader way, examining how what they do fits in to the library's vision, it still is valuable to have a designated individual who is responsible for looking at what is being done across the organization and trying to bring all of the library's community interactions together in an organized fashion. This person, the community partnership development director, should be perceived by library staff as neutral, not favoring one or the other library department. Establishing a new position in administration that has these responsibilities will make it easier for the library to sustain an active partnering program. Developing a new position does not necessarily mean adding additional staff to the library, which can be a difficult point to argue in the face of tight budgets. At the Williamsburg Regional Library, the community partnership development director position was initially established by shifting a librarian who was the main person working on partnership development from the Adult Services Department into library administration. A new position did not need to be created, but the appearance of interdepartmental neutrality was established.

A final advantage to establishing a new administrative structure for partnership development is that it allows the library to approach partnering not just as reactive decision making but proactively, with more librarywide coordination of future activities. Partnership development can be a positive tool to help libraries remain vital to their communities. Your library will derive the greatest benefit from partnerships that are developed in a thoughtful, coordinated fashion, working across library departments. To be successful, partnering must be part of the ongoing planning process for the library, and the creation of administrative structures to support partnership development's central role are essential to its success.

What Might the Structure Look Like?

Taking on partnership development as a primary tool for achieving the library's vision will probably mean some changes in how planning and decision making are done at your library. These changes will ultimately result in a stronger institution, as partnership development demands that library departments work more closely together not just on specific projects but in looking toward the future.

We have found two structural changes most helpful in creating a positive atmosphere for partnership development. The first was the creation of the position of community partnership development director. The second was the establishment of the Community Partnership Development Group (CPDG). Both of these facets of the structure enhance the librarywide nature of partnership development and encourage the use of partnering by all library departments when appropriate.

The community partnership development director is part of the library's management team. The position description states that, "Under the supervision of the Library Director, the Community Partnership Development Director plans, organizes, and implements methods and procedures for conducting a comprehensive, library-wide community partnership development program. Chairs the Community Partnership Development Group. Participates in the planning and evaluation of programs, services, and goals for the entire library through the management team and other committees." The community partnership development director takes on a number of essential functions, including

- leading the library's community partnership development process as guided by the library director, the CPDG, and the library's strategic plan;

- planning, organizing, and implementing methods and procedures for staff to use to develop and manage partnerships;

- working with departments to create partnerships with civic and nonprofit organizations, educational and government entities, businesses, and libraries to reach new user groups, to expand access to library services, and to further shared library–community partner goals;

- consulting with staff on the partnering process to include visioning, planning, negotiating, implementing, documenting, and the evaluation of initiatives;

- chairing the library's CPDG;

- developing community contacts to encourage library-partnership initiatives and to promote the assets and strengths of the library;

- maintaining a database of library–community relationships to facilitate a librarywide approach to partnership development;

- developing and implementing techniques to evaluate library–community partnerships in light of specific project goals, departmental goals, and the library's strategic plan;

- coordinating and conducting partnership development skill building training;

- with the library director, determining specific partnerships to manage; and

- participating in the planning and evaluation of library programs and services through the management team and other committees and through individual development to improve the quality of library services.

These essential functions outline two areas of influence for the community partnership development director. The first, and most important, role is internal. The community partnership development director is responsible for making sure that there is a coordinated and consistent process within the library for developing and tracking partnerships across the institution. We have discussed in previous chapters how successful partnership development relies on interdepartmental cooperation and a strong vision of where the library is going. The community partnership development director's role is to encourage this sort of effort through building up policies and procedures for partnership development at the library.

In later chapters we further explore the specific processes in establishing, documenting, and evaluating partnerships. In all of these steps, the community partnership development director plays an essential role in representing the library as in institution. The community partnership development director has an advisory role, in some way serving as counsel to the library's partnership managers. She advises staff who are considering establishing partnerships on the specific procedures to follow. She guides the development of partnership proposals and presents those proposals to the library director and the CPDG. She also guides the crafting and review of all letters of agreement, and may participate directly with the community partner to facilitate the process.

The community partnership development director's second role is external. She is the "big picture" person at the library. She needs to have a substantial awareness of the community and of the opportunities that the community affords the library. She must have a strong command of what the library brings to the table in a partnership. She then uses this information to assist staff in developing partnerships and also in working with the CPDG to prioritize partnering possibilities.

Once our library selected partnering as an important tool for achieving its vision, it became clear that there should be some sort of group with in the library that would bring together representatives from all departments to work on partnership development issues (a CPDG). Initially, our CPDG comprised staff from all levels within the institution, from shelvers to department heads. In the initial stages of partnership development, this seemed to be a useful way to get staff on board with the concept of partnering and to generate excitement about partnering throughout the library. Before long, though, we realized that this group needed to be able to make decisions that affected the work of all library departments. This would not be possible unless the department heads were a part of the decision-making process, and the makeup of the group changed to reflect this need. Members of our CPDG represent all of the public service departments in the library. The library director and assistant director are also members of the group, as is the development director. The CPDG is chaired by the community partnership development director.

The CPDG is charged to

> facilitate a strategic and integrated approach to partnering with civic and nonprofit organizations, educational and government entities, businesses, and libraries to reach new user groups, to expand access to library services, and to further shared library–community partner goals. The work of the CPDG will be guided by the goals of the library's current strategic plan.
>
> The CPDG will generate ideas that may be accomplished by one department, or by collaboration among departments. The CPDG will also facilitate communication among departments to forestall potential confusion in the community about what individuals represent the library in various endeavors.
>
> The CPDG will annually evaluate the effectiveness of WRL's community partnership efforts."

The CPDG takes on several responsibilities. This group makes recommendations on specific partnership proposals. When a staff member has come up with a potential engagement or marriage, he or she drafts a partnership proposal (see figure 4.1), with the help of the community partnership development director. This document is then circulated to the CPDG for discussion and comment. At this point, the members of the committee can raise their concerns, ask for further clarification on specific issues, and suggest other possible pieces for the proposed partnership. (See proposal review questions in the box.)

Figure 4.1. Partnership Proposal Review Form

DEVELOPMENT OF A LIBRARY ENGAGEMENT OR MARRIAGE

The attached development form should be filled out when PROPOSING THE FORMATION of an engagement or marriage between the library and a community partner. This development form is a tool to help you assess the appropriateness, suitability and benefits of a POTENTIAL partnership for the library. All proposed engagements and marriages should help the library achieve the 2002–2005 Williamsburg Regional Library (WRL) Strategic Plan. For assistance in completing this form, and other related questions, please contact the WRL Community Partnership Development Director. Completed proposal forms will be reviewed by the Community Partnership Development Group.

EVALUATING LIBRARY ENGAGEMENTS AND MARRIAGES:

The library forms community partnerships to achieve specific goals: to reach new users, to reach library users in a new way, to tap into community assets and strengths, to gain support for library resources/programs, to gain valuable feedback, and to create new resources. An engagement or marriage is successful if it helps the library achieve one or more of these goals. Below are some project measurement tools that should be kept in mind as you prepare this partnership development form.

GOAL 1. Reach new users

Survey	new user registrations	program evaluation form	interviews or focus groups	program attendance figures

GOAL 2. Reach library users in a new way

Survey	number of circulations	program evaluation form	interviews or focus groups	program attendance figures

GOAL 3. Tap into community assets and strengths

List of, and $ value of assets/strengths	program attendance figures	survey	interviews or focus groups	

GOAL 4. Gain support for library resources/programs

survey	program attendance figures	new user registrations	number of circulations	monetary contribution

GOAL 5. Gain valuable feedback

survey	interviews or focus groups	program attendance figures	program evaluation form	

GOAL 6. Create new resources

monetary contribution	number of circulations	website hits	lists of created resources	

Figure 4.1. (*Cont.*)

Williamsburg Regional Library Partnership Proposal Form

Your name:

Your department:

Proposed community partner(s):

Proposed project details:(attach a separate sheet if you need more space)

1. Will the partnership reach new users?

____ Definitely ____ Somewhat ____ No ____ Not Sure

On a scale of 1 to 10 (with 10 being most important) please rate the importance of reaching new users for this proposed partnership project:

1   2   3   4   5   6   7   8   9   10

What tool(s) will you use to measure if the partnership has helped reach new users?

Estimate how many new users are anticipated to be reached and explain how they will be reached:

2. Will the partnership project reach library patrons in a new way?
____ Definitely ____ Somewhat ____ No ____ Not Sure

On a scale of 1 to 10 (with 10 being most important) please rate the expected importance of reaching library patrons in a new way for this partnership:

1   2   3   4   5   6   7   8   9   10

What tool(s) will you use to measure if the partnership has reached new users?

Explain the anticipated way in which patrons will be reached:

Continued →

Figure 4.1. (*Cont.*)

3. Will the partnership project tap into community assets and strengths?

____ Definitely ____ Somewhat ____ No ____ Not Sure

On a scale of 1 to 10 (with 10 being most important) please rate the expected importance of tapping into community assets and strengths for this partnership:

1   2   3   4   5   6   7   8   9   10

Describe the anticipated community assets and strengths that will be tapped into through this partnership:

4. Will the partnership gain support for library resources/programs?

____ Definitely ____ Somewhat ____ No ____ Not Sure

On a scale of 1 to 10 (with 10 being most important) please rate the expected importance of gaining support for library resources/programs for this partnership:

1   2   3   4   5   6   7   8   9   10

Explain the anticipated support to be gained for library resources/programs:

5. Will the partnership enable the library to gain valuable community feedback?

____ Definitely ____ Somewhat ____ No ____ Not Sure

On a scale of 1 to 10 (with 10 being most important) please rate the expected importance of gaining community feedback for this partnership:

1   2   3   4   5   6   7   8   9   10

Describe how you plan to measure the anticipated feedback about the library:

Figure 4.1. (*Cont.*)

6. Will the partnership create new library resources?
   ___ Definitely ___ Somewhat ___ No ___ Not Sure

On a scale of 1 to 10 (with 10 being most important) please rate the expected importance of creating new library resources for this partnership:

   1   2   3   4   5   6   7   8   9   10

List what resources you expect to create:

Can the library create this resource without forming this partnership?

7. What library resources (staff time, money, equipment, staff expertise) will you need to support this partnership?

8. Please list the possible effects this partnership project might have on other WRL departments.

9. How does your proposed partnership contribute to the library's vision for 2005 and fit with the library's strategic plan and your department's current implementation plan?

10. What benefit(s) will your community partner derive from this potential partnership?

Partnership Proposal Review Questions

The following questions are used by the Williamsburg Regional Library's Community Partnership Development Group to review partnership proposals submitted by staff or departments:

- Does the primary interest of the proposal fit with the WRL mission statement?

- Are WRL's values compatible with the work that will be undertaken?

- Does the proposal contribute to the library's vision of 2005 and fit with the library's strategic direction?

- How will the partnership benefit the library?

- What resources (e.g., time, money, materials, equipment, staff expertise) might be available for the partnership?

- Is there someone who can represent the library in developing this partnership, and can that person be spared at this time?

- How much time will it take, and how will that time connect to other library activities?

- Is there any reason why the library would not wish to be involved?

- Does another group in the community do this better?

Once the CPDG members have made comments and suggestions, the proposal may need to go back to the library staff member who developed the idea. The proposal will undergo further revision with the assistance of the community partnership development director. Following these revisions, the proposal is again routed to the CPDG, and if there are no major changes suggested, then the proposal is forwarded, with the sanction of the CPDG, to the library director, who has final approval of all new engagements or marriages. This sort of discussion and comment can be facilitated by carrying it out electronically via e-mail.

In addition to making recommendations to the director on specific partnership proposals, the CPDG is also charged with examining how the library implements partnership development throughout the institution. The group should meet regularly throughout the year (the Williamsburg Regional Library's CPDG meets quarterly). These meetings offer group members an opportunity to share partnering activities in each department, to discuss procedural issues, to explore new opportunities for partnering, and to assess any partnership proposals that are in process. Regular meetings, and sharing of the information from those meetings with all library staff, reinforce the importance of partnering within the institution.

The CPDG has the responsibility for exploring the community with an eye toward partnership development. Each year the group should look at trends, opportunities, and changes in the community to establish what possibilities these may create for community partnerships. The CPDG creates an annual list of these trends and opportunities for partnership development in the community and incorporates that into its partnership implementation plan. (See the next box for an example of a partnership implementation plan from the Williamsburg Regional Library, including the trends and opportunities list.) This assessment of the community portrait becomes a useful tool for each department in the library as annual work plans are developed. The items on this list are those that the CPDG sees as areas that may be ripe for partnership development, and individual departments may wish to explore them in the coming year.

FY04 Partnering Implementation Plan

Partnering with community organizations and businesses will continue to be an emphasized strategy for the library during FY 2004. The Community Partnership Development Group (CPDG) recommends departments follow the priorities listed below when developing new partnerships during FY 2004. Also provided are a list of trends, changes, and opportunities that may impact our community partnership development activities. An asterisk indicates an opportunity that is viewed by the CPDG as a priority for FY2004.

Reasons WRL partners with the community and priorities for FY2004

High priority

- Reach new users

- Tap into community assets and strength

- Gain support for library resources/programs

Medium priority

- Gain valuable community feedback

Lower priority

- Create new resources

Trends, changes, and opportunities impacting partnering in FY2004

- $11,000,000 fewer dollars will come into Williamsburg

- Williamsburg-James City County Public School—Library partnership*

- Third high school in Williamsburg-James City County

- Ukrop's agreement and their desire for new initiatives*

- Department of Motor Vehicle—state mandates effecting libraries*

- Social Services (Food Stamps program)—mandate*

- Library of Virginia—pre-school training initiative

- Library of Virginia—Tech Riders computer training

- Sharpe Program—literacy course

- Sentara Williamsburg Community Hospital embracing the Planetree model of patient-care emphasizing patient information*

- Gates Foundation computer support ends

- Verizon's Mobile Internet Learning Center grant support ends

- Williamsburg Community Health Foundation receiving a large infusion of money for community health care*

- Hispanic and other limited English speaking population increasing

- Thomas Nelson Community College to build a Williamsburg campus opening in 2006

- James River Elementary School—strategically located facility is under-enrolled

- New leadership in the community—York County library director, chairman of the JCC Board of Supervisors, Colonial Williamsburg Foundation library director.

- Wal-Mart opens in Lightfoot area

- 2004 is an election year

- 2007 Jamestown celebration

- William and Mary Public Policy Department –Geriatric Institute planned

- American Homes 2000+ housing development in James City

- Area bookstores—knowledgeable marketing strategies

- Virginia Employment Commission increases traffic

- International workers during summer at Busch Gardens and with other area employers.

- Budget crisis—roller coaster concern with budget will continue

- James City County agencies

- College of William and Mary's Earl Gregg Swem Library remains under construction *

- Senior services—Historic Triangle Senior Center *

- AARP Tax Aide program moves into the library as a waiting space

- All Together—a new director and a new direction*

As well as surveying the changing face of the community portrait, the CPDG should also examine internal partnership issues. As your library gets into the process of partnering, you will undoubtedly find that procedures and policies need to be adjusted or modified, and the CPDG is where these discussions take place.

Another mission for the CPDG is to determine annually which of the six reasons for partnering will be the focus for the library in the coming fiscal year. Designating these reasons as high, medium, and low priority sets some direction for the departments as they begin their planning for each new year. If the CPDG is diligent in assessing the community portrait, it should be easy to use this understanding in setting partnering priorities.

Roles in Partnership Development

As we noted at the beginning of the chapter, a well-developed internal structure for partnership development does four things: it generates ideas; it helps to set priorities; it assists in managing individual partnerships; and it coordinates partnering librarywide. Library staff at different levels have parts to play in each of these areas. We have discussed the responsibilities of the community partnership development director and the CPDG; now we will look at each of the four areas that are supported by a formalized structure and see how all staff participate in this structure.

Generating Ideas

- Library staff

  - Seek out ideas for potential library–community partnerships through community contacts

  - Work with department head and/or the community partnership development director to explore ideas within the context of the library's strategic plan

  - Document community contacts in whatever form the library has chosen to use

  - Look for and assess opportunities for interdepartmental cooperation

- Partnership managers

  - Explore opportunities for expansion or new directions that may arise in existing partnerships

  - Look for and assess opportunities for interdepartmental cooperation

  - Look for library–community partnership opportunities

- Department heads

  - Look for and assess library–community partnership opportunities

  - Make partnering an important part of the department's annual implementation planning process

  - Look for and assess opportunities for interdepartmental cooperation

- Community Partnership Development Group

  - Set library's annual partnering priorities, as discussed above

  - Generate ideas for partnerships that may be accomplished by one department, or by collaboration among departments

- Community partnership development director

  - Develop community contacts to encourage library-partnership initiatives and to promote the assets and strengths of the library

  - Look for and assess library–community partnership opportunities

- Library director

  - Develop community contacts to encourage library-partnership initiatives and to promote the assets and strengths of the library

  - Look for and assess library–community partnership opportunities

- Library board

  - Share ideas for potential library–community partnerships

  - Develop community contacts to encourage library partnership initiatives and to promote the assets and strengths of the library

Description of the Roles of Those Involved in the Williamsburg Regional Library Partnership Program

IDEAS
   Library Staff
   Partnership Manager
   Department Head
   Community Partnership Development Director
   Library Director
   Board of Trustees

APPROVAL
   Community Partnership Development Director
   Community Partnership Development Group
   Library Director

ADMINISTRATIVE
   Administrative Assistant
   Partnership Manager
   Department Heads
   Community Partnership Development Director
   Community Partnership Development Group
   Library Director

To clarify for staff how a partnership idea proceeds through the library's internal structure, we devised a flowchart of the process (figure 4.2). The chart tracks the progress of an idea for an engagement or a marriage from its conception through the implementation of the partnership and signing of a letter of agreement.

Coordinating the Development of Partnering Librarywide

The broad view of partnering at the library is really established by four groups within the institution.

1. The *library board* develops and supports a strategic plan to outline the library's mission and vision, and then designates partnership development as an important tool in achieving these goals.

2. The *library director* shapes partnering at the institution by approving specific partnerships, by approving procedures for partnership development, and by making sure that all library departments are actively looking at partnering as a strategic tool. This is not to say that all departments must be developing lots of partnerships. In fact, one of the director's roles is to select the engagements or marriages that make the most strategic sense for the institution. However, all departments do need to be open to the possibility of partnerships as a mechanism.

3. The *Community Partnership Development Group*, guided by the library's strategic plan facilitates a strategic and integrated approach to partnering, as discussed above. The CPDG also promotes communication among departments to forestall potential confusion in the community about what individuals represent the library in various endeavors. Finally, the CPDG annually evaluates the effectiveness of the library's partnering efforts (not individual partnerships, but the entire process).

4. The *community partnership development director* leads the library's partnering efforts by developing and establishing procedures for partnership development; by chairing the partnership development group; and by being the focal point both in the library and in the community for partnership development.

Figure 4.2. Developing a Partnership Proposal

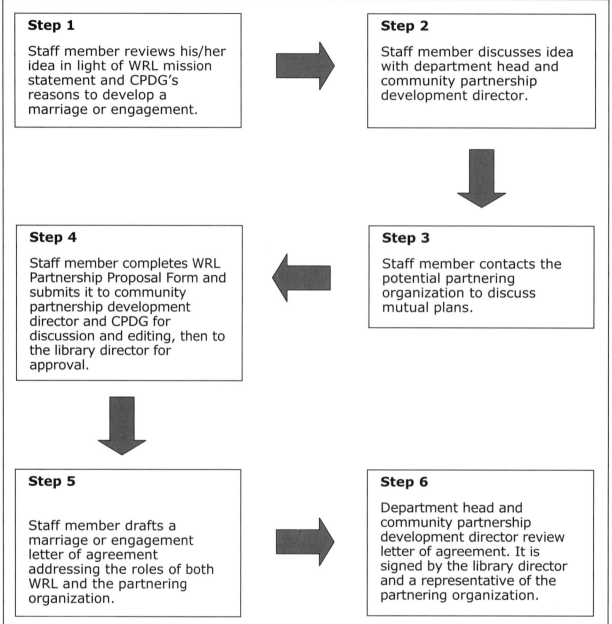

Step 1

Staff member reviews his/her idea in light of WRL mission statement and CPDG's reasons to develop a marriage or engagement.

Step 2

Staff member discusses idea with department head and community partnership development director.

Step 4

Staff member completes WRL Partnership Proposal Form and submits it to community partnership development director and CPDG for discussion and editing, then to the library director for approval.

Step 3

Staff member contacts the potential partnering organization to discuss mutual plans.

Step 5

Staff member drafts a marriage or engagement letter of agreement addressing the roles of both WRL and the partnering organization.

Step 6

Department head and community partnership development director review letter of agreement. It is signed by the library director and a representative of the partnering organization.

Keep in mind that partnering is not an end in itself but a tool for achieving the library's vision. With this in mind, it is evident that partnering priorities—with whom the library is going to partner—flow out of the library's strategic plan and mission. The ties to the strategic plan and mission mean that the setting of priorities for partnership development will necessarily arise out of the library's administrative team. Within the structure we suggest, there are roles for a variety of administrative staff in this process. The CPDG, the community partnership development director, department heads, the library director, and the library board all play a part in prioritizing partnerships.

As outlined previously, the CPDG plays several roles in setting partnering priorities. First, the CPDG annually discusses and prioritizes changes and trends in the community that could affect existing partnerships or offer new partnering opportunities. Using this information, the CPDG gives guidance to individual departments by establishing which of the six reasons for partnering will be priorities in the coming year. As the individual departments begin to plan for the coming year, they use these priorities to establish what sort of partnering initiatives they will pursue. Finally, the CPDG makes recommendations to the director on specific engagement or marriage proposals.

The community partnership development director's role in setting priorities is twofold. She works within the library to plan, organize, and implement methods and procedures for staff to use to develop, manage, and evaluate partnerships. In this position, the partnership director sets the internal priorities in terms of the partnering process. That is, she determines how things are done. The partnership director also chairs the library's CPDG. She is the person in the library who lives and breathes partnering. This role puts the partnership director in the position to shape partnership development by working both with partnership managers and with library administration.

Department heads are responsible for determining how partnering fits into their departments' needs and directions, as well as thinking how they can work collaboratively with other library departments. They work with staff to establish the priorities for the department and then look at ways that partnering can be used to achieve those priorities. It is essential that the heads of the public service departments serve on the CPDG. These are the departments that are most likely to be involved in establishing community partnerships. Department heads need to buy in to the concept and process of partnering as a strategic direction. Without their cooperation, partnership development will be impossible. The department head must convey the importance of partnering as a strategic direction to staff and guides the department's annual implementation planning process as it relates to the partnership strategy.

The library director's role in establishing partnering priorities is also twofold. First, the director creates an environment that fosters the establishment of partnership development and supports that development as an important direction for the institution. This sends the message to all library staff that building community relationships through partnering is a strategic direction for the library in carrying out its mission. Second, the library director has the final approval of all new partnerships. This allows the director to determine library partnership priorities with respect to community and local government issues. There may be cases where a potential partnership meets all of the necessary library criteria but for political reasons cannot be established. For example, a potential community partner may have a good relationship with the library but a poor relationship with one of the library's funding bodies. In this case, the library director may decide that it is better for the library not to pursue the relationship until the political climate has changed. It is the responsibility of the library director to make these decisions.

Finally, the library board has a role in setting partnering priorities. By approving the library's strategic plan and monitoring its progress, the library board is accepting the idea of partnership development as a priority for the institution. The library board will also set library policies and provide budgetary resources to facilitate the development of the library's partnership program. There will be a variety of levels of board participation in actual partnering decision making, depending on what sort of relationship exists between the library and its board. Some boards may seek a level of involvement in partnership development that could include setting guidelines for library staff or being more directly included in the decision-making process. Other boards will take a more hands-off approach, allowing library staff to carry out their responsibilities within the strategic directions established and approved by the board.

In either case, it is crucial to the success of partnership development that the library board be kept informed of how the partnering process is working. Without the support of the board, it will be difficult for library staff to make the commitments to community partners that a successful partnering program demands. So be sure to make board members aware of what is going on with partnership development at your library. Let them know about marriages and engagements that have been established and how these relationships are helping the library to achieve its vision.

Library board participation in partnership development may become more direct in relationships that involve financial decisions or legal contracts. The relationship between library boards and the library director will vary from institution to institution. Direct board participation in partnering will depend on how much authority the library director has been given to enter into financial agreements. Similarly, when partnerships involve the creation of a legal contract between the library and the community partner, the library board may expect to be more closely involved in the process. In these cases, which will be rare, library policies or structures may require library board approval of the contractual relationship or even require that the board sign off on the contract. It is important to be aware of what expectations your library board has regarding its role in partnership building at the library and to be able to shape the structure to include board participation if necessary.

Managing Partnerships

Setting up an internal structure for partnering lays the foundation for consistent management of library partnerships. As noted above, the community partnership development director is responsible for developing procedures for partnership management, in consultation with the partnership team and the library director. These procedures cover the responsibilities of partnership managers, both in developing a partnership and in coordinating an ongoing relationship.

The partnership manager acts as the main point of contact between the library and the community partner. The manager becomes the focal point for the construction of a trust-based relationship between the two organizations. This trust is built, as in any relationship, through careful and straightforward communication, responsiveness to the partner's needs and interests, and a shared excitement about what the partners can achieve together. Setting up internal mechanisms for partnering helps to ensure that the library's partnership managers are all approaching their partnerships with the same understanding of what partnering is and how it works within the library.

We discuss in other chapters much of the day-to-day work done by partnership managers: developing a partnership from an idea to a formal arrangement, matching missions, crafting a letter of agreement with a community partner, evaluating ongoing marriages, and tracking contacts to build a community portrait. By developing a structure that supports and codifies these roles, we have given partnership managers and those staff who are considering a possible partnership a firm foundation from which to operate.

The internal structure also ensures a more consistent approach to partnering throughout the library. Partnership managers can potentially come from any department in the organization and from any level within that department, from support staff to department head. Often, because of their roles in library administration, higher level staff have a clearer picture of how partnering operates at the library. A clearly developed set of procedures and policies regarding partnership development makes it easier for frontline staff to become involved in partnership development by establishing the important pieces of the process and tying them into the library's mission and vision.

5

Forming a Partnership

Exploring the Community

Forming successful community partnerships requires that the library make reasoned choices among the many potential partners in the community. These choices will be based on a variety of factors, including the needs of the library, the needs of the prospective partner, the potential partner's mission and values, the resources that the partner would bring to the relationship, and the partner's reach into the community. To make these choices for your library it is necessary that the library staff have an understanding of the community. By bringing together a variety of views of the community, as discussed below, the library staff develops a portrait of its community that will enable participants to make intelligent choices regarding possible community partners.

There are a number of ways that you can prepare library staff to "troll" the community in an organized fashion for potential community partners. First, the community must be defined geographically. In public libraries, the geographic setting is usually determined by the sources of funding, and may be a city, a county, or some combination of the two. Other libraries will need to set the bounds of the community in which they plan to seek partnerships. Clearly defining the area in which the institution will look for partners will give staff who are interested in developing partnerships some guidance. It will allow the library to quickly turn down or give lower priority to partnership opportunities that come from organizations outside the focus area. As pointed out in chapter 1, the trend in partnering in both the business and public sectors is toward local partnerships. The large national partnerships that were common initially in the partnership movement have proven less successful in meeting company needs and have often proved too large to manage effectively. Partnering will be more effective and will better meet your library's needs if you act locally to seek out potential partners. Local groups have an understanding of and commitment to the community that may not be found in larger regional or national organizations. At the same time, local groups have a stake in the community that a regional or national organization may not have. This is not to say that partnerships with larger institutions cannot be successful, but larger partners must be chosen with care to ensure that their interest in the partnership reflects and addresses your local needs, and that decisions are made and priorities set at a local level.

In exploring the community for potential partners, it is important that the library not simply be reactive. It can be easy to fall into the habit of only exploring partnering opportunities when the library has already been approached by an outside organization. However, the most successful partnering program is created when the library has a clear awareness of its mission and vision as well as its assets and strengths, as discussed in chapter 3, and then uses that awareness to actively seek out community partners who will help the library achieve its goals. It is also important to remember that assessing and exploring the community is an ongoing process. It is not something that you do once at the beginning of developing a partnering program and then set aside. Successful partnering depends on you and the library continually maintaining an awareness of community trends and directions and building on this awareness to establish the most fruitful partnerships.

One of the first mechanisms that you can use for developing and maintaining an awareness of community trends and directions is to look within your current library staff and see who belongs to or is involved in some way with community-based groups. Often the library director, management staff, and library board members have connections with other community organizations that may be potential partners. These people may sit on boards of community groups, participate in service organizations, or volunteer with public sector institutions. All of these relationships allow you the opportunity to gain an insider view of what is going on in these segments of the community.

In addition to the administrative staff, the rest of the library staff also may have these sorts of connections, and you should make sure not to overlook the value of having frontline staff contribute to the library's understanding of the community portrait.

In previous chapters, we emphasized the importance of developing a librarywide awareness of and appreciation for the importance of partnering to the success of the library. We suggest that the best partnering programs involve staff at all levels of the institution in the process of developing a strategic plan and vision, creating a list of the library's assets and strengths, and identifying potential partnership opportunities. If your library follows these suggestions, it will be easier to move from the theoretical to the concrete and to involve staff in surveying the community for potential partners. You should encourage all staff to participate in this ongoing community assessment by providing opportunities for them to share their knowledge of the community and by actively encouraging this sharing process.

If your library has set up a formal partnership development group as outlined in chapter 4, one part of this group's mission should be to regularly assess the opportunities for partnership development within the community. This requires knowledge of community directions. On an annual basis, this group should have its members outline what they see as the trends, changes, and opportunities in the community that will affect partnering possibilities in the coming year. The resulting list should offer a portrait of the community that suggests where the library's partnering efforts should be directed in the coming year.

This procedure can be expanded to other library staff by having departments in the library engage in a similar process as they work on developing individual departmental work plans. Within the individual departments, the list of opportunities can be used to prioritize what the department might achieve through partnering. In addition, the individual departmental lists should be reported back to the partnership development group and made part of the group's annual portrait of the community. Expanding the evaluation of trends, changes, and opportunities to the entire library broadens the final community portrait and, again, encourages staff acceptance of the value of partnering as a tool for institutional success.

Many of the techniques that the library uses for exploring the community for partnering opportunities are the same as those that would be used in developing strategies for marketing and library development. The important thing here is to keep partnering in the forefront and not let the community exploration diverge from this focus.

There are some obvious mechanisms for keeping abreast of community trends, changes, and opportunities. Encourage library staff to read the local papers, especially the smaller community-focused weeklies or biweeklies. These resources are an excellent way to keep up with who is doing what in the community, because they generally have a very narrow coverage. If possible, subscribe to enough copies of the local paper to support easy staff access. Awareness of local trends and changes can be made a part of the expectations for all staff in the library. Doing so will reinforce to staff that the library places a high value on this sort of knowledge.

In chapter 1 we cite Susan Goldberg's *Library Journal* article on the importance of connecting the "leadership circles" of the library to those in the community.[1] We would go a step further here and assert that the library should not only work to connect existing leadership circles but also actively seek to position staff in these leadership circles in the community. There are many opportunities for staff at all library levels to become involved in the local community. Again, this reinforces the position of the library in its community, but also, and more important for partnership development, it allows these staff members to bring back to the library a better understanding of the trends, changes, and opportunities for partnering that exist in the community. The library should encourage staff to take active roles in community organizations, in schools, and, when appropriate, in local government. Staff members who are involved in community interactions, whether as a part of a community organization or simply in keeping up with community changes through reading and conversations, should be thinking with each of these interactions, "What is the potential here for the library?"

Building this kind of awareness among staff is not an easy process and not one that will happen immediately upon entering into partnership development. It requires that the library communicate to staff the expectation that they actively participate in keeping aware of community trends, changes, and opportunities, and it requires a further commitment from the library that those staff members who do develop this awareness and use it to further the partnering effort will be rewarded.

Another mechanism for keeping up with the trends and changes that are occurring in the community is for library staff to develop regular contacts with organizations, neighborhood groups, and local coalitions. These contacts are not necessarily focused on developing new partnerships, but rather are part of the process of developing a community portrait that will aid you in choosing potential partners for the library. As part of the partnership planning process for each new year, library staff can make "house calls" on selected community organizations to see what plans these groups have in place for the coming year. Again, this is not so much to suggest to these groups that the library wants to develop a partnership, though this may ultimately be the result. Instead, this should be a matter of the library staff simply gathering information that will shape the library's response to community trends.

Conversations of this sort can be a very useful way to pick up information on community trends. For instance, in discussion with a local supermarket employee, one library staff member learns that a new product line of foods aimed at the Hispanic market is going to be added in the coming year. In combination with information gathered from other organizations, this knowledge may assist you in planning library services to non-English speakers. It also alerts you to the possibility of reaching a new user community through a community partner.

One concern that may arise in this process is that some groups may be suspicious of why library staff are coming to find out what they are doing in the coming year. They may feel that the library is seeking to take ideas from them rather than seeking to share information or collaborate. You must allay these fears by assuring the organization that you are simply trying to develop a more accurate community portrait. Also, you must be willing to share your library plans and ideas with the group. (The bibliography lists a number of titles on coalition building that will be useful in this process.)

As part of the process of developing a community portrait, you will want to take advantage of the library's association with local government officials. To be successful, libraries need to have a strong, positive working relationship with their funding bodies. This relationship has implications across the spectrum of library issues, from funding to collection development. Like the library, local governments have a mission to serve all of the community. As a result, they are often an excellent source of information about community trends and changes. Library staff should cultivate positive connections with local government staff that will enhance the library's access to this information. In many cases, this role will fall to the library director as the main liaison between the library and local government, but it is by no means limited to the director alone. All library staff can develop connections to local government agencies that will benefit partnership development.

In addition to providing anecdotal information on trends and changes in the community, local governments can often be an excellent source of hard data on the community that can be added to the partnering picture. Frequently, local governments are able to provide access to community data that can be combined with library data to provide new light on the role of the library in the community. As an example, the Williamsburg Regional Library staff worked with local government and college staff to develop a GIS (Geographic Information Systems) map that overlaid the location of library card holders onto a map of our primary service area. The resulting map gave the library a much clearer picture of what areas in the community are not currently taking part in library services, and it encouraged us to prioritize partnering efforts to reach into those underserved areas. Other government information such as census data and planning projections provides a wealth of information for the library about community trends, changes, and opportunities for partnering.

Awareness of local cycles is another essential piece to developing a community portrait that will assist the library in exploring and evaluating potential partnerships. There are a wide range of cycles in the local community that overlap, and being aware of how they work and intersect will allow the library to approach potential partners at opportune times in their cycles. At the same time, there may be possible partnerships that will be rejected because it is impossible to match the organization's cycle with the library's cycle.

Community Cycles

- **Budget cycles:** All organizations, the library included, operate within the constraints of the fiscal year. However, not all fiscal years are on the same calendar. For planning purposes, you should be alert to organizations that are not on a similar schedule for budgeting. Working in partnership with organizations whose budget cycle differs requires increased flexibility from both partners, as well as careful communication.

- **Legislative cycles:** It is essential for libraries to be aware of legislative cycles, especially at the local and state levels. These cycles include elections, budget creation, legislative sessions, etc. All of these cycles will have an effect on trends in the community, and they may offer opportunities or compel you to seek out library partners in the community.

- **Planning cycles:** An excellent source for information about trends and opportunities in the larger community is the planning process that local governments take up periodically. It is important that you be aware of comprehensive planning cycles, as the entire process will lay out new directions for the community. In addition, during the development of the plan, library staff can glean a great deal of useful information about the current portrait of the community. Keeping aware of citizen input and reaction to the comprehensive plan is also an excellent tool for you to build awareness of trends in the community.

- **Fund-raising and grant cycles:** Fiscal year cycles are not the only monetary cycles in the community that should be monitored as part of the partnership development process. You should also be aware of fund-raising and grant cycles.

- **Educational cycles:** Since educational institutions offer many opportunities for partnership development, and since these institutions are important community gatekeepers, you should make sure that you keep track of the cycles that revolve around the educational year. These include both planning and budget cycles.

By taking the time to carefully explore the local community—defining the geographic bounds; identifying community leaders; connecting library staff with the circles of leadership in the community; annually assessing trends, changes, and opportunities in the community; building strong relationships with local government; and developing an understanding of community cycles—you will be able to establish a comprehensive community portrait that will be a firm foundation for developing successful long-term cross-sector partnerships.

Matching Plans to Opportunities

Once you have developed at least the beginnings of a community portrait, and with it, an understanding of potential community partners, the next step is to begin matching your library plans to the opportunities. This step involves narrowing down the information that has been gathered in the community assessment and focusing your library's partnering efforts based on that information. Prior to initiating contact with a potential partner, you will need to do some background work, evaluating the possibilities of a partnership with a specific institution. It is important to remember not to over-prepare this sort of background research. Partnering is an art and not a science, and often the decision to begin discussion with a possible partner will depend as much on the feel that the library staff have for the possibilities as on exhaustive research. Nonetheless, it is important to have some sense of who or what the potential partner is prior to beginning formal discussions.

As we have emphasized in previous chapters, some sort of strategic plan is essential to successful partnership development. Selecting potential cross-sector partners is where the library's strategic plan and partnering intersect. The plan gives those library staff who are responsible for selecting and developing partnership guidance about where the library wants to go in the next several years. Partnering is the mechanism that will allow the library to get there. The plan gives guidance to what the library wants to achieve, when it wants to achieve these goals. Then by looking at the community portrait developed as described above, you can select whom you hope to work with to make your library vision a reality.

After a potential partner has been identified, the first step in proceeding toward a formal relationship should be to explore the organization's corporate culture. One of the first questions you should ask is, "What is the mission of the potential community partner?" Many organizations post their mission statement and core values on their Web site; and the Internet can be a useful tool in developing a picture of a potential partner. It is often more difficult to locate information on smaller organizations about their directions and goals, and it is here that you must take advantage of the various tools and processes mentioned previously in this chapter—local papers, personal contacts, etc.—to get a feel for the values of a possible partnering organization.

In addition to considering the mission and goals of the potential partner, there are other aspects that are equally important to consider when beginning to look at a specific partnering opportunity:

- What is the organization's position in the community?

    - Does the organization serve a large or small segment of the community?

    - Does the organization have other partnerships in the community?

    - Does the organization have an existing relationship with the library, through dates, for example?

- Who are the groups or segments of the community that the potential partner serves?

    - Does the organization offer the library opportunities to reach a new user group?

    - Does the organization offer the library the chance to reach current users in a new way?

- What sort of resources might this organization bring to the relationship?

    – Does the organization offer the potential to develop new resources?

    – Does the organization do things that the library cannot do?

- What are the organization's strategic directions?

    – How do these directions match the library's strategic directions?

    – Are there directions that clash with the library's values and mission?

- What is the reputation of the organization in the community?

    – Will a relationship with this partner strengthen the library's position in the community?

    – Are there potential issues with this organization that may have a negative effect on the library's standing in the community?

- Who are the leaders in this organization?

- Does the timing seem right?

- Are unique opportunities arising?

Potential Conflicts in the Matching Process

As the library begins to try to match missions with potential partners, it is useful to keep in mind some of the conflicts that can occur in the process. Many of these conflicts can be resolved during the discussion and negotiation stages of forging a partnership, but there may be times where a formal partnership is not possible.

One of the most common conflicts in the partnering process occurs when you are trying to develop a relationship with an organization whose mission clearly does not match that of the library. This sort of problem frequently arises when beginning to work with organizations in the for-profit sector. While many businesses espouse the importance of giving back to the community, at the same time, they are also primarily focused on making a profit for their owners and shareholders. It is certainly possible for the library to form a fruitful partnership with a business, but it does require careful assessment of how the two institutions' missions fit together.

Trying to match up planning, funding, and budget cycles with a possible partner is also an area of potential conflicts. During the initial discussions with a prospective partner make sure that you both are clear about how the other's cycles operate. As the partnership moves forward into setting specific goals and objectives, each partner must be aware of how these plans will fit into the other partner's planning and fiscal cycles. This sort of conflict may arise with any potential partner but can usually be worked out through careful discussion and setting of goals.

When working with smaller nonprofit groups there are a number of issues that may cause conflicts. Often smaller groups operate on a fiscal shoestring and will look to a relationship with the library to supplement budget needs. These groups are not in a position to offer the library much in return. Just as it is essential for the library to understand its assets and strengths (see chapter 3), it is important to develop a clear picture of what strengths the prospective partner brings to the table. Becoming involved in a one-way liaison is to be avoided. These groups may be doing valuable work in the community and would benefit from additional funds. However, a potential partner must be able to offer more to the relationship. A successful partnership involves both partners adding value to the relationship.

As a result of budget constraints, smaller nonprofit groups may have internal structures that do not lend themselves to successful partnering efforts (high staff turnover, poor communication, unclear hierarchies). These sorts of problems are by no means limited to smaller organizations though, and the library will want to be wary of developing relationships with groups whose internal structure is chaotic. It is very difficult to establish the kind of communication links that are necessary for successful partnering if the staff in the organization are constantly turning over. While an organization that has constant staff turnover generally does not make a good partner, be careful not to eliminate organizations that are in a state of change as prospective partners. Often, a period of institutional change creates opportunities for new thinking and new directions, and it can be useful to approach a possible partner at this time. However, it is important to discuss possibilities with people who are in a position to actually act on the discussions.

One source of conflict in developing partnerships arises from not dealing with the right people in the potential partner's organization. It is not always necessary to deal with the director or president of a potential partner. It is important, however, to have this individual's agreement that the organization should pursue the relationship with the library. When opening your discussions with a prospective organization, you need to deal with staff who are in a position to make decisions and to put those decisions into effect. Starting off too low in the hierarchy of the organization may lead to problems when promises are made that cannot be kept or resources are offered that are not really available.

Political considerations are also part of the partnership picture, and they may lead to conflicts. If your library receives funding from local governments, you need to be sensitive to how the relationships that you seek out will appear to the local funders. If you are seeking to develop a partnership with an organization that has been at the center of local political controversy, problems may develop. The Waco-McLennan County (Texas) Library System experienced the political realities of working with outside organizations in October 2002. Planned Parenthood agreed to pay the library system several hundred dollars per year to provide access to its collection of reproductive health and sexuality materials. Anti-abortion protestors criticized the agreement, and according to an article in the *Library Journal,* "Waco City Manager Kathy Rice said that, in the future, if the library wants to catalog materials from nonprofit agencies—Planned Parenthood agreed to pay a few hundred dollars a year to do so—approval of both the city council and the library board will be required."[2]

Choosing High-Priority Partnerships

Once the library has listed its strengths, developed a portrait of the local community, and identified prospective partners, there may be a tendency to go out and try to develop lots of partnerships at all levels: dates, engagements, and marriages. Initially this is not a bad thing, as it takes advantage of staff enthusiasm about partnering and can build a sense of excitement in the library about the process. However, it will soon become evident that to sustain a partnering program over the long term, it is necessary to set priorities for partnership development. Using the criteria outlined in previous chapters, each potential partnership must be considered to see how it fits in the library's strategic plan, what the purpose for this partnership is, what the partner will bring to the relationship, what commitments the library will be making, and how the partnership will operate over the long term. In chapter 4 we discuss the decision-making roles within the library as they relate to partnership development. The staff in these positions will have the responsibility to evaluate each potential partnership and select only those partnerships that will further the library's mission.

Selecting partnerships is by no means a science. Once the research has been done, and the initial discussions have occurred, making the decision to proceed with formalizing a relationship at the level of an engagement or marriage is as much based on whether the relationship feels right for the library and the partner as on any hard figures that can be derived. As in a real engagement or marriage, initiating a partnership involves a leap of faith, based on a sound understanding of the prospective partner. You can only know so much about the partner, and based on that knowledge you make a decision to work to build a relationship.

Opening Discussions with a Potential Partner

The facets we have discussed thus far apply to all levels of partner relationships. When you identify a potential long-term relationship, it is time to begin discussing formalizing that commitment. The initial discussion should be focused on developing an ongoing relationship, not simply on a specific project. In terms of the analogy set forth in chapter 2, you should be looking at an engagement—a long-term commitment—not a one-night stand. Keeping the focus on the relationship rather than on a specific event or project can also be an asset in convincing potential partners that you are not simply out to get something from them. Some organizations may be suspicious of your motivations and reluctant to commit. In initial conversations, it is crucial to show the potential partner how by building a formal relationship your two organizations can create something that is bigger or better than either could do alone.

Here is where a good understanding of the potential partner's mission and standing in the community will be essential. In the process of discussing forming a relationship, it will be up to the library to point out to the potential partner where the missions of the two organizations intersect and how this relationship will further the goals of both institutions. Ultimately, there must be some sort of hook that brings the two institutions together and that will serve to keep them together over the course of the relationship. There can be many reasons that make partnering desirable for both the library and a potential partner:

- To work jointly on solutions to specific problems or issues

- To create something that could not easily be created by one or the other institution (sharing costs, resources, staff time, etc.)

- To combine expertise or knowledge

- To blend common goals or activities

- To make more efficient use of limited resources

- To eliminate duplication

- To increase influence in the community or build political clout

There are several things to consider when setting up the initial discussions with a prospective partner. Most important, decide who should be at the meeting. Who are the gatekeepers in the partnering organization? Who has the decision-making authority? As noted previously, make sure that the person or persons with whom you are meeting have the ability to make some decisions for the organization. The partner's representatives should have enough responsibility in the organization to be able to clearly describe what the organization can and cannot do and to indicate what they are looking for out of the partnership. They do not have to have the authority to make a final decision, but they do need to be in direct contact with those who do have this responsibility.

Before the initial meetings with a potential partner, library staff need to make sure that they have their story straight. That is, all staff involved in the partnering discussions should have a fluent understanding of the library—what it has to offer, what it is trying to achieve, and what this partnership can do. Without this understanding, it is impossible to develop partnerships that will meet the needs of the library, and it will be difficult to conduct fruitful negotiations with a potential partner.

We have devised a basic toolkit of items that library staff who are working on partnership development need to be able to talk with purpose to a prospective community partner.

The Partnership Discussion Toolkit

To make the best decisions when talking to a potential partner, the library staff must have a clear understanding of and ability to articulate the following points. These are not items about which you can tell a prospective partner, "Oh, I am not sure about that, but I can look it up." The staff negotiating partnerships must be able to bring this information readily to mind, without hesitation:

- The library's mission, vision, and core values

- The plan for where the library is going, both short-term and long-term

- Who the library serves

- Basic library statistics—circulation, collection size, patron base, number of card holders, electronic resources, etc.

- Current programs and services at the library

- Annual operating budget

- Information about library staffing—numbers, departments, command structure, qualifications, etc.

- Funding and administrative board structures—names of library board members, Friends board directors, etc.

- Role of volunteers in the library—How many are there, and what do they do?

- Other library partners

- Partnership program requirements

A potential partner will probably not need to know all of this information, and you should be careful not to overload an organization you are courting with too much data. However, a clear understanding of all of these points will allow the library staff who are negotiating a partnership to make the best decisions about what to offer and what to expect in return.

There are some questions that seem to come up frequently when discussing a relationship with a potential partner. If you take the time to consider how you would answer the following questions, in addition to having the information discussed above readily available, you will be able to make the most of the initial partnership discussions.

- Why should we form a partnership?

   – What is the need this relationship would meet?

- What are the benefits for each partner?

- Who else would benefit from this partnership?

- How will the library support the relationship?

- Are the timing and political climate right for this relationship to move forward?

- Why a partnership and not some other arrangement?

- What are the best and worst case scenarios for this relationship?

Prior to meeting with a prospective partner take some time to think through how you would answer each of these questions. If you have been careful in identifying a possible partner, utilizing the tools and techniques described in previous chapters, the answers to these basic questions should be easy to come up with. If you find it difficult to answer any of these questions, you may wish to reconsider why you want to partner with this particular institution.

It is also important to have some idea of what the end result of these initial meetings will be. Early on, the goal may simply be a clarification of the opportunities that exist, or a commitment to continuing to explore these opportunities. It is important to have an idea of what you want to get out of a partnership relationship prior to meeting with a prospective partner. At the same time, be sure that during the initial meetings you are open to changes and opportunities that arise from the discussion. As the relationship begins to form, the meetings should have more concrete results: developing plans, setting goals, and finally creating a formal partnership agreement.

Notes

1. Susan Goldberg, "Community Action Now: Defying the Doomsayers,." *Library Journal* 118 (March 15, 1993): 29.

2. Andrew Albanese et al., "Waco-McLennan County Library System," *Library Journal* 127 (December 2002): 24.

6

Letters of Agreement

One of the most important elements in a successful partnership program is the documentation of each individual marriage or engagement with a formal letter of agreement. To extend the marriage analogy, the letter of agreement is the partnership equivalent of a prenuptial agreement. It lays out the expectations from each partner, and while it usually will not include contingencies in case of divorce, it does try to assess roles and responsibilities and will cover monetary issues as well. The letter of agreement is an opportunity for both partners to flesh out the who, what, when, where, and why of the relationship. It lays the foundation for the partnership and provides a communication tool that will prove useful in the evaluation of the partnership.

There are two types of partnership agreements that can be drafted, legal contracts or nonbinding letters of understanding. On the whole, the letter of agreement or understanding is the simpler tool and preferable to use whenever possible. It does not need the services of an attorney to draft and is much less threatening to present to a partner. There may be occasions, though, when the complexity of the proposed relationship would warrant a legal contract between the two organizations. In particular, if the partnership involves large sums of money, joint staffing or other personnel issues, licensing agreements for electronic resources, or one institution providing direct services for the other it is probably a good idea to consider a legally-binding contract. In a larger partnership that has a variety of initiatives, and perhaps a variety of partners, there may be some items that would need to be covered in a legal contract and some that can simply be part of a letter of agreement. Some instances where a legal contract may be needed are partnerships that involve substantial shared fiscal responsibilities, such as joint funding of materials purchases or shared positions. Partnerships where one partner is taking over specific functions for the other partner may require a contract for services to be developed. Partnerships that include major contracting of space by either partner may also require a legal contract.

Most library partnerships can be documented with a simpler letter of agreement. These types of documents can have several different names, depending on the preferences of the partners. They can be called letters of agreement, partnership agreements, letters or memoranda of understanding, or goals and programs. Each community partner will have different institutionally based concepts of what title appeals the most to them, and the library should be sensitive to the partner's preference. Regardless of the name given to the document, the most important thing is to get it written. Some prospective partners will be concerned about the idea of drafting any sort of document that has a semblance of being a contract. In these cases, language can be inserted in the agreement that clearly states that the agreement does not constitute a legally binding contract. (See figures 6.1 through 6.5 at the end of the chapter.)

Writing a useful letter of agreement is a time-consuming process. In addition to requiring the time of the library partnership manager to draft the document, the process of getting agreement between the library and the partner on the contents can be slow. Nonetheless, it is a valuable document to have in hand, and well worth the effort. The partnership agreement sets the framework for a long-term relationship. One of the most valuable roles that the letter of agreement has is as a communication tool. This role is important both externally (between the partners) and internally (within the library).

One of the most important functions of the letter of agreement is to set up the lines of communication and to clarify responsibilities between the partners. A well-crafted letter of agreement should minimize misunderstandings among the organizations in the partnership about what each organization's roles and obligations are within the partnership. The partnership agreement will also clearly define the communication procedures between the two partners.

In particular, the agreement should identify the key staff members in each organization who will be responsible for communicating with the other organization during the life of the partnership. For simpler partnerships, this is usually the role of the partnership manager, who takes on the day-to-day administration of the activities relating to the relationship. More complex partnerships, having multiple initiatives and projects, may also have several staff members for each organization heading up different parts of the whole. In these cases, the partnership agreement should present a communication plan to delineate which staff members from each of the partner organizations will be responsible for working on each different initiative. There may also be partnerships that are managed by teams of staff from one or both of the partners. In these cases as well, the communication channels outlined in the letter of agreement will contribute to the overall success of the relationship.

In addition to setting the framework for the entire partnership relationship, a letter of agreement provides a number of other benefits that make it worth the effort required to develop it. The letter of agreement communicates the partnering program to the community in a very public way. It is a tangible result of the partnering process. Examples of existing partnership agreements can be shown to prospective partners to give them a sense of what sort of expectations a partnership with the library will involve. The letter of agreement can also be used to illustrate to library boards and funding bodies the success of the partnering program. Finally, the letter of agreement demonstrates to library staff the value that the library places on the partnering process as a tool to achieve its goals.

When working with potential partners, especially those who have approached the library unsolicited, partnership agreements documenting existing relationships can serve as a helpful filtering device. The time spent developing a letter of agreement shows the seriousness with which the library takes the entire partnering process. Organizations that are not really ready or lack the resources to enter fully into the requirements of a formal partnership (an engagement or marriage)—clearly defined goals, shared risks and benefits, and well-established communication processes—will be likely to shy away from involving themselves in a relationship that requires the level of formalization indicated in a partnership agreement. They may prefer just to date.

Within the library, there are additional benefits to formalizing partnerships with a letter of agreement. As noted previously, the letter of agreement enumerates the responsibilities within the library for coordinating and managing the various aspects of the partnership. Not only does this set up a mechanism to ensure that projects are carried out, it also emphasizes the cross-departmental nature of almost all partnership projects. While drafting the partnership agreement, the community partnership development director circulates the draft to all the departments that will be affected by this new relationship.

This draft process gives any department the opportunity to raise concerns or ask for more clarification on the partnership. Since the partnership has already been approved by the library administration, this should not be viewed as an opportunity to scuttle the entire project. Rather, it requires the partnership manager to coordinate the partnering initiatives in a librarywide fashion rather than working piecemeal. Partnerships often arise out of the library's public service departments. Circulation, reference, children's services, program services, and bookmobile departments have the most connections in the community, and in general are more directly in contact with potential partners. The drafting of the partnership agreement can be especially helpful in reinforcing the important roles that support departments (information technology, technical services, facilities, etc.) play in the library. It can be easy to overlook the impact of a relationship with an outside organization on these departments. When the draft of a partnership agreement is circulated among the various library departments, staff members can raise concerns about their role, and these questions can be addressed before they become problems during the implementation phase.

Table 6.1 lists some of the Williamsburg Regional Library's partnerships and indicates which departments are involved. As you can see, many partnerships involve several library departments.

Table 6.1. How Departments Support Selected Partnerships

Community Partner	Adult Services	Automated Services	Bookmobile	Circulation	Facilities	Program Services	Technical Services	Youth Services
AARP Tax Aide	X	X			X			
Backstage Productions					X	X		X
College of William & Mary Swem Library	X			X		X		
Colonial National Historical Park	X			X		X	X	
James City County Neighborhood Connections	X		X	X	X		X	
Sentara Williamsburg Community Hospital	X	X	X	X	X	X	X	X
Williamsburg Area Learning Tree	X			X	X	X		
Williamsburg James City County Schools	X	X	X	X	X	X	X	X

A formal partnership agreement can also be used to promote partnership development within the library. The letter of agreement defines how the goals of the partnership tie into the library's strategic plan, as can be seen in figures 6.1 through 6.5. Making the letters of agreement accessible to all library staff gives those staff considering working on developing a partnership a guide to the library's expectations for partnerships.

Finally, a well-drawn up letter of agreement is essential to the process of evaluating the partnership. During the evaluation, both partners can use the letter of agreement to establish whether goals have been accomplished, communications have been clear, and initiatives carried out. In each of these cases, a clear understanding of the expectations allows the partners to easily determine whether the relationship has been a valuable one. In addition, the letter of agreement serves as a starting point for developing new initiatives and goals to be outlined as the relationship develops from year to year. Drafting and signing a new letter of agreement on a regular basis (annually, biennially, etc.) keeps the partnering relationship focused.

Writing a Letter of Agreement

There are a number of elements that each letter of agreement will have in common and that you will want to include in whatever sort of written document you use to track partnerships. (For examples of actual letters of agreement, see figures 6.1 through 6.5.) The list below identifies the elements that are important to include in a partnership agreement, in the order that we have found most useful. Obviously, each institution will want to create a letter format that will most effectively comprise the elements it feels are most valuable.

Common Elements in Letters of Agreement

- **Identification of the partnering organizations:** Although this is usually the library and one partner, there may be letters of agreement that involve several partners. For example, the Williamsburg Regional Library has developed a partnership with two historical parks in the community, the Association for the Preservation of Virginia Antiquities and the Colonial National Historical Parks. The letter of agreement that was drafted for this relationship includes both partners in the same document.

- **Date of the agreement:** For purposes of tracking relationships and for keeping communication clear, it is important to date the letter of agreement.

- **Disclaimer:** If necessary, this is the place to include a disclaimer that clarifies that the letter of agreement is not a binding legal document.

- **Mission matching:** Drawing on language from each of the partners' mission statements, this section lays out why these two organizations feel that a partnering relationship is valuable, based on similar missions.

- **Goals statement:** This statement defines the purpose of the partnership. It should reflect both goals that each institution wishes to achieve individually from the partnership as well as the shared goals of the relationship. In this statement, you are clarifying what the partners want to do together and why they want to do it. This is not necessarily the place to list all of the projects and initiatives that the partners will be undertaking.

- **Initiatives:** A smaller partnership that has only one or two initiatives can list them immediately after the enumeration of the goals. For a partnership involving multiple initiatives, these should be listed in an attachment to the agreement.

- **Statement of responsibilities:** This section lays out the obligations that each of the partners will be taking on within the partnership. It should be quite specific about each partner's areas of responsibility. Some of the headings for different responsibilities are:

    - **Resources:** What will each partner contribute in terms of staff time, money, or other resources?

    - **Facilities:** Is there going to be joint use of facilities? Are there limits to the use of one partner's facilities by the other partner?

    - **Promotion and publicity:** Who will be responsible for the various aspects of promoting the partnership? It is a good idea to include a statement here that indicates that each partner will pass drafts of promotional material by the other partner to ensure that there is joint control over the message being given to the public.

    - **Evaluation:** What is the period for the evaluation?

    - **Communication statement:** Who are the contacts for the partnership in each organization? Are there specific communication paths that should be followed?

    - **Timeline:** What is going to be achieved by when? The timeline helps to focus the particular projects and initiatives of the partnership by putting end dates on them. This will also be helpful in the evaluation process.

There are some optional elements that may be useful in certain partnerships. The more complex a partnering relationship grows, the more likely it is that you will want to have some of these elements in the agreement. Often these elements are more useful as attachments to the actual letter of agreement rather than imbedded in the agreement itself. Optional attachments to the letter of agreement may include the following:

- **Communication plan:** In a complex partnership that involves several staff members from each institution as part of the management team, it helps to have a detailed communication plan attachment. This document should include not only the names of various contacts but also information on who in each institution is responsible for particular initiatives.

- **List of agreed upon programs:** In a partnership that has a strong programmatic piece, it is valuable to develop a list of specific events that will take place over the course of the partnership term. For example, the letter of agreement for the Williamsburg Regional Library's partnership with a children's theater company lists all of the performances to take place each year as part of the partnership. A list of agreed upon programs helps prevent "mission creep" in a partnership, where an enthusiastic partner wants to keep adding on new elements throughout the year.

- **Timeline:** Again, for a smaller partnership it may be possible to include the timeline within the actual letter of agreement. However, a partnership that involves multiple initiatives spread out over a period of time will benefit from drawing up a clear timeline that sets out the dates for all of the responsibilities in a separate document.

- **Details of initiatives:** In a complex partnership that features a number of initiatives, it can be helpful to both the partnership manager(s) and others in the institutions to draft a document that gives the details of each specific initiative. This will be useful in preventing misunderstandings about goals and responsibilities as the partnership progresses. It also lets both institutions clearly see the energy and resources they are going to have to expend to sustain the partnership.

- **List of each institution's strengths:** This attachment makes clear to staff in each institution what the other is offering as part of the partnering relationship.

- **Mission statements:** Attaching the full text of each organization's mission statement to the partnership agreement allows those not directly involved in the partnership (board members, funding bodies, staff) to see where the missions match.

- **Budget statement:** If the partnership involves substantial fiscal responsibilities for one or both partners, it is essential to put these responsibilities into an attachment. Although, as discussed previously, the letter of agreement is not a legally binding document, delineating the fiscal responsibilities can prevent problems with misunderstandings about money down the road.

- **Fiscal limitation statement:** In a partnership that includes jointly funded initiatives, consider including a statement that provides flexibility should unanticipated budget concerns preclude a partner's ability to fund an initiative. A fiscal limitation statement should be used judiciously, not as an escape clause for bad planning or poor communication.

- **Divorce clause:** If there are shared facilities, budgetary responsibilities, staff, etc., as part of the partnership, it is probably a good idea to clearly define how these factors will be handled if the partnership does not work out.

Issues and Potential Problems with Letters of Agreement

The letter of agreement is an important communication tool for focusing the partnering effort and addressing potential areas of conflict between partners. Nonetheless, it is not always easy to get the process done. A typical problem that will be faced in getting a partnership documented is the reluctance of library staff to engage in the process. This reluctance may arise from a feeling that drafting a formal letter of agreement is too time-consuming, or that it is just another hoop to jump through. Other staff may not see the need to document "things that we have always done." In both of these cases, the partnership director should explain to the staff members the importance of the documentation process, and how, in the long run, a carefully crafted letter of agreement will save the time of the partnership manager by preventing misunderstandings between the partners as well as between library departments involved in the initiatives.

When creating a letter of agreement the library may have to confront reluctance on the part of the potential partner to the process. Often this arises because of concerns about the legal nature of the agreement. To overcome this sort of hesitation it is perfectly appropriate to change the name of the document or to include some sort of disclaimer in the text that clarifies that it is not a legally binding document.

At other times, the reluctance of a potential partner to participate in the development of a letter of agreement may be based on a feeling that it is not important to the relationship. In these cases, the potential partner's reluctance to codify the relationship should encourage the library to reexamine the relationship. It may be that this partner's reluctance is a symptom of larger problems that could develop as the relationship proceeds, and the library may want to rethink the partnership.

Another issue that arises in developing a letter of agreement concerns who actually writes the document. Our experience has been that the library staff who are managing the particular partnership are best placed to draft the letter of agreement. These staff members should have the clearest understanding of the relationship and have worked most closely with the potential community partner. As part of the drafting process, the staff writing the document should consult with the library's community partnership development director. This person helps guide the partnership manager(s) through the process and brings a librarywide point of view to the process. The director can point out initiatives or goals that will affect other departments in the library and can facilitate communication on these areas between the partnership manager and the affected departments.

Timeline for Developing a Letter of Agreement

It is important to remember that drafting a letter of agreement may be a slow process, particularly for the first iteration. Agreements in future years usually proceed much more quickly, because the framework, format, language, and processes have been established. The letter may have to go through several drafts with the library and then take into account any comments, concerns, or suggestions that come from the partner. If the partner needs to have the letter of agreement vetted by legal staff, which may occur particularly with government agencies or large organizations, that can delay the process even more. It is not essential that the letter of agreement be completed and signed prior to beginning planning with a community partner, or even prior to carrying out initiatives. It is important that the development of the letter of agreement not be set aside in favor of doing these other things.

Following are the steps we have found typical in developing a letter of agreement with a potential community partner:

1. Based on discussion and negotiation with the prospective community partner, the library staff person who will be managing the partnership works with the library community partnership development director to draft the letter of agreement. This process allows the library to retain control of the procedure. The community partner reacts to the document, but the library staff create it.

2. The draft document is presented by the community partnership development director to all library departments that will be affected by the creation of this new partnership. At this time, the departments can comment on the initiatives and raise any questions or concerns that they have regarding the relationship.

3. The draft document then goes to the library director, who can also raise questions and concerns about the prospective relationship. These questions may go back to the department heads or to the partnership manager for resolution.

4. As the draft document is reviewed in steps 2 and 3, it may go through a number of revisions, adding and removing sections and reworking the language. Following these revisions, the appropriate staff should once again review the document.

5. Once the appropriate library staff have made comments and the letter of agreement has reached a final draft stage, it goes to the prospective partner for review and comment. Depending on how much priority the partner gives to the relationship, and also depending on the number of people in the partner's institution that need to see the document, this process can take time.

6. Following the partner's review, the managers from the two institutions meet to discuss any changes or additions to the letter of agreement.

7. Again, as in step 4, the process of revising the letter of agreement with the partner may involve several drafts being created.

8. Once the final drafts are finished and all accompanying attachments approved, two originals of the letter of agreement are signed by the library director and then sent to the partner for a signature. It is best to have the library director sign first, because we have found that this accelerates getting the community partner's signature.

9. Finally, one signed document is retained for each partner's files. The community partnership development director distributes photocopies of the original as necessary.

Renewing a Letter of Agreement

Renewing a partnership essentially involves the same steps described above for developing a letter of agreement. It should prove to be a faster process, as much of the infrastructure will be the same from year to year. However, each time a partnership is renewed, it provides a good opportunity to look at the partners' missions and the goals of the relationship to see if there is still a good match and the necessary commitment. During the renewal process, the partners should plan on evaluating the success of the collaboration. (We discuss the actual evaluation process in chapter 7.) Because the evaluation and renewal of a partnership will take time, the partners should agree on a logical point to start the process. If possible, schedule the renewal process at a time when other partnership activities have slowed down. This gives both partners ample time to review the relationship. The Williamsburg Regional Library's partnership with the AARP Tax Aide to provide tax assistance to the community goes through the renewal process in May and June, following the rush of the January to April tax season. Choosing this time for renewal also allows more advance preparation for planning new initiatives in the coming year.

Not every partnership needs to be reviewed annually. Based on the goals of the partnering relationships, the level of commitment required by both partners, and the sense of matched missions, there may be partnerships whose renewal period is even as long as two or three years. However, it is important not to let partnerships go on too long without review.

Figure 6.1. Williamsburg Regional Library, Colonial National Historical Park, and the Association for the Preservation of Virginia Antiquities Partnership Agreement

WILLIAMSBURG REGIONAL LIBRARY, COLONIAL NATIONAL HISTORICAL PARK, AND THE ASSOCIATION FOR THE PRESERVATION OF VIRGINIA ANTIQUITIES

PARTNERSHIP AGREEMENT

GOAL: On behalf of the Williamsburg/James City County community, the organizations listed on this agreement will work together to; (a) promote the library as a place where patrons can learn about the local historical and natural environment; (b) promote Historic *James*towne and Yorktown Battlefield as places to study and enjoy its history and natural resources; and (c) promote - by educating the public - the parks' historical significance. Through the partnership, the library and park have created new resources and seek to reach park and library users in new ways. To reach these goals, the partners will collaborate in the ways listed below. This agreement will be reviewed by **December 31, 2003**.

Partnership Coordination:
Williamsburg Regional Library (WRL): Adult Services Assistant
Colonial National Historical Park, Jamestown (CNHP): Chief Historian
Association for the Preservation of Virginia Antiquities (APVA): Historic *James*towne Program Coordinator

Continued →

Figure 6.1. (*Cont.*)

Promotion/Publicity Responsibilities	
WRL	**CNHP/APVA**
• Provide library resource guides for special events such as Yorktown Day, Jamestown Day, Bacon's Rebellion, Archaeology Month, Native American Month and First Assembly Day.	• Provide materials advertising special park events that relate to specific park pack topics.
• Promote the partnership and the park packs to library patrons through displays, posters, newsletters and other outreach efforts.	• Promote and advertise the availability of park packs and the partnership through posters, newsletters, and other outreach efforts .
• Review all NPS/APVA promotion pieces related to WRL during production and prior to final distribution	• Review all WRL promotion pieces related to CNHP/APVA during production and prior to final distribution.
• Promote CNHP/APVA through a link on the WRL website	• Promote WRL through a link on the CNHP/APVA website
Resources/Facilities Responsibilities	
WRL	**CNHP/APVA**
• Distribute CNHP/APVA materials related to special park events through the patron information racks and community bulletin boards at both libraries.	• Provide a speaker for library presentations highlighting park special events and park pack topics.
• Provide meeting room space (not including the e-CLIC room or WL Theatre) for special presentations by CNHP/APVA related to special park events and park pack topics, no more than two times a year.	• Provide materials for any special displays at the library.

Continued →

Figure 6.1. (*Cont.*)

Partnership/Evaluation Responsibilities	
WRL	**CNHP/APVA**
• Provide evaluation forms (paper and WRL website) for park pack users to provide feedback.	• Provide a certificate and/or badge at the park to visitor's completing the park pack activities.
• Explore other potential park pack topics and/or ways this partnership might develop.	• Explore other potential park pack topics and/or ways this partnership might develop.
• Work with CNHP/APVA to annually evaluate the partnership agreement.	• Work with WRL to annually evaluate the partnership agreement.

Williamsburg Regional Library	**Colonial National Historical Park**
___(signature)___	___(signature)___
Library Director Williamsburg Regional Library	Chief Historian Colonial National Historical Park
	Association for the Preservation of Virginia Antiquities
	___(signature)___
	Historic *Jamestowne* Program Coordinator Association for the Preservation of Virginia Antiquities

Figure 6.2. Williamsburg Regional Library and James City County Neighborhood Connections Partnership Agreement

WILLIAMSBURG REGIONAL LIBRARY (WRL) and JAMES CITY COUNTY NEIGHBORHOOD CONNECTIONS (JCC-NC)

PARTNERSHIP AGREEMENT

OCTOBER 2002

This Partnership Agreement is not a legal contract. It is a letter of understanding between the Williamsburg Regional Library (WRL) and James City County Neighborhood Connections (JCC-NC) to state the goals of the partnership and to enumerate the project responsibilities for each party.

GOAL:

WRL and JCC-NC are forming a partnership to achieve the following three goals: 1) to improve public access to a collection of materials that was originally housed at JCC-NC and which had limited access by the community in that location; 2) to reach new library users, especially those potential users who are residents of at-risk neighborhoods within James City County; and 3) to enhance the working relationship between the Library and James City County by promoting the new collection and the partnership.

WRL and JCC-NC will work together as community partners to accomplish these goals by acquiring, cataloging, circulating, and promoting the "Neighborhood Knowledge" collection of print and audio-visual materials that will be housed at the James City County Library (JCCL). The "Neighborhood Knowledge" collection contains homeowners association items and related materials such as information on pet regulations, insurance, legal liability, contract law, and management issues.

Continued →

Figure 6.2. (*Cont.*)

Project Responsibilities:

Resources:

Williamsburg Regional Library

- Acquire, catalog, shelve, and circulate collection of print and audio-visual materials that comprise the "Neighborhood Knowledge" collection.

- Make a notation in the Dynix field by the Technical Services Department that the materials are part of the "Neighborhood Knowledge" collection for circulation statistics purposes.

- Create research pathfinders for the "Neighborhood Knowledge" collection and for related online resources.

- Meet with the JCC-NC representative on a semi-annual basis to review circulation statistics of the "Neighborhood Knowledge" collection and to assist in the acquisition and de-acquisition process for materials.

- Register attendees at JCC-NC training sessions for library cards.

JCC Neighborhood Connections

- Provide WRL with library and audio-visual materials that comprise the "Neighborhood Knowledge" collection.

- Maintain a reference-only duplicate set of the "Neighborhood Knowledge" collection and house it at JCC-NC.

- Support the "Neighborhood Knowledge" core collection financially by ordering and paying for new materials annually for an amount not less than $300.00.

- When new or standing-order library materials arrive at JCC-NC, they will be forwarded to JCCL with a notation to the Technical Services Department that the materials are for the "Neighborhood Knowledge" collection.

- Utilize the JCC-NC member discount for purchase of new library and audio-visual materials.

- Act in consultation with the WRL librarian regarding acquisition and de-acquisition of library and audio-visual materials for the "Neighborhood Knowledge" collection.

Continued →

Figure 6.2. (*Cont.*)

Facilities:

Williamsburg Regional Library

- Provide meeting room space at the library during normal library hours for JCC-NC related educational programs free of charge and as space is available.

- Library staff will have the opportunity to participate in these educational programs and to promote the "Neighborhood Knowledge" collection.

- There will be no more than four JCC-NC related educational programs held in library facilities per year, and the Williamsburg Library Theater and the eCLIC room at JCCL are not included in the available rooms.

- Provide equipment for use in the library for educational programs.

- Provide technical support for educational programs.

JCC Neighborhood Connection

- JCC-NC guest speakers will leave the room in the same condition as they found it and each room will be used on a self-serve basis.

- JCC-NC will incur all costs associated with speakers' fees, if any, and costs associated with educational materials and handouts.

Continued →

Figure 6.2. (*Cont.*)

Promotion:

Williamsburg Regional Library	**JCC Neighborhood Connections**
• Review all JCC-NC promotion pieces related to the collection or to WRL during production stages and before final distribution.	• Review all JCC-NC promotion pieces related to the collection or to JCC-NC during production stages and before final distribution.
• Promote JCC-NC through a link on the WRL web site.	• Promote WRL through a link on the JCC-NC web site.
• Promote the "Neighborhood Knowledge" collection and its relationship to JCC-NC in the WRL newsletter four times per year.	• Promote WRL and the "Neighborhood Knowledge" collection orally at its quarterly and annual training sessions.
• Promote the "Neighborhood Knowledge" collection by creating and disseminating research pathfinders to library patrons.	• Promote WRL by disseminating research pathfinders created by the Library for the "Neighborhood Knowledge" collection during training sessions.
• Contribute half of the cost for production of the research pathfinders created by the Library.	• Contribute half of the cost for production of the research pathfinders created by the Library.
• Promote JCC-NC by directing interested library patrons to contact or to visit JCC-NC directly for further information.	• Promote WRL and its resources through the JCC-NC newsletter.
• Place a book sticker in each of the "Neighborhood Knowledge" materials indicating its origin from JCC-NC.	• Promote WRL and its resources through library information brochures distributed at individual homeowner's association meetings.
• Provide WRL promotion pieces to JCC-NC for distribution at individual homeowner association meetings.	• Work with WRL to explore other avenues for promotion on an annual basis.
• Work with JCC-NC to explore other avenues for promotion on an annual basis.	

Continued →

Figure 6.2. (*Cont.*)

Evaluation/Partnership:

<u>**Williamsburg Regional Library**</u>

- Partners will evaluate the program and the terms of the agreement annually in accordance with the end of the fiscal year.

- A semi-annual review of circulation statistics for the "Neighborhood Knowledge" collection will be conducted by WRL and a meeting held with the Director of JCC-NC to discuss acquisition and de-acquisition of library materials.

- Provide standard WRL Program and Library Service evaluation form.

- Work with JCC-NC to implement the timeline.

<u>**JCC Neighborhood Connections**</u>

- Partners will evaluate the program and the terms of the agreement annually in accordance with the end of the fiscal year.

- Provide statistics on attendance at quarterly and annual training sessions.

- Provide statistics on attendance at educational programs held at the WRL classroom facilities.

- Assist WRL in getting attendees to complete a program evaluation form.

- Work with WRL to implement the timeline.

Continued →

Figure 6.2. (*Cont.*)

Program Coordination:

- WRL and JCC-NC will designate appropriate representatives to work as a team to plan, coordinate, promote and evaluate this partnership.

- The contact person for the Williamsburg Regional Library will be Adult Service Department, Community Services Librarian. The contact person for James City County Neighborhood Connections will be the Director.

Continued →

Figure 6.2. (*Cont.*)

Implementation Timeline:

November 2002

- Partnership Agreement review is completed by both parties and Agreement signed.

- Library and audio-visual materials that comprise the "Neighborhood Knowledge" collection are catalogued and shelved at the James City County Library

- Room reservations are made for the fall educational programs given by JCC-NC.

- Library research pathfinders for the "Neighborhood Knowledge" collection are created by WRL and distributed to JCC-NC.

December 2002

- Publicity regarding the "Neighborhood Knowledge" collection is disseminated in the fall JCC-NC newsletter.

- A link to JCC-NC is implemented on the WRL web site.

- A link to WRL is implemented on the JCC-NC web site.

January 2003

- Meeting between the Community Services Librarian and the JCC-NC Director regarding circulation statistics for the "Neighborhood Knowledge" collection and discussion regarding acquisition of library materials.

- Publicity regarding the "Neighborhood Knowledge" collection is disseminated in the January WRL newsletter.

February 2003

- Research pathfinders and WRL information packets assembled for JCC-NC annual meeting to be held in March 2003.

June 2003

- Begin evaluation process of partnership by both parties using circulation statistics of "Neighborhood Knowledge" collection, feedback from JCC-NC training sessions and educational programs, and any other relevant anecdotal information.

- Review Partnership Letter of Agreement.

Continued →

Figure 6.2. (*Cont.*)

Williamsburg Regional Library	**Neighborhood Connections**
___(signature)_____	___(signature)_____
Library Director Williamsburg Regional Library	Director JCC Neighborhood Connections
Date:	Date:

Figure 6.3. Williamsburg Community Health Foundation and Williamsburg Regional Library Partnership Agreement

---

WILLIAMSBURG COMMUNITY HEALTH FOUNDATION (WCHF) and WILLIAMSBURG REGIONAL LIBRARY (WRL)

FUNDING RESEARCH CENTER PARTNERSHIP AGREEMENT

July 2003

This Partnership Agreement is not a legal contract. It is a letter of understanding between the Williamsburg Regional Library (WRL) and the Williamsburg Community Health Foundation (WCHF) to state the goals of the partnership and to enumerate the project responsibilities for each party.

Goal: WRL and WCHF will work together as community partners to develop and maintain the Funding Research Center (FRC) for use by community agencies to be located at the Williamsburg Regional Library. The FRC will (a) enrich resources available to area residents; (b) offer materials in a range of formats to satisfy community needs; and (c) expand WRL's role in teaching the community how to access and evaluate information.

Continued →

Figure 6.3. (*Cont.*)

PROJECT RESPONSIBILITIES:

WILLIAMSBURG COMMUNITY HEALTH FOUNDATION

Funding

- As funding is available, provide funds for the purchase of supplementary materials to enhance FRC collection.
- As funding is available and appropriate, provide additional support to augment WCHF PBF interest income.
- As funding is available and appropriate, and additional materials are identified to enhance the collection, WCHF will consider adding funds to the PBF.

Promotion/Recognition

- Link to FRC on WCHF web site.
- All WCHF prepared promotional and publicity materials related to FRC reviewed by WRL prior to final distribution.
- Publicize FRC information in WCHF publications annually, as appropriate.
- Annual co-sponsorship of FRC workshop and FRC session during the Grantsmanship Center Inc. session (if invited).
- Promote the FRC and WRL training to community health and human services agencies through mailings.

Partnership/Evaluation

- The Partnership Team will work together to develop an annual timetable for implementation, promotion and evaluation.
- Annual evaluation of project and partnership.
- Commitment to ongoing partnership.

WILLIAMSBURG REGIONAL LIBRARY

Resource Access

- Provide space in Williamsburg Library for FRC print materials.
- Acquire, catalog, shelve and circulate printed materials that comprise the FRC.
- Update core FRC and related resources biennially, or as funds are available.
- Adult Services librarians assist patrons guided by Reference Desk service standards.
- FRC web page: Project Manager will design, select and maintain annotated links as part of the WRL web site.

Promotion/Recognition

- Link to WCHF from FRC web page.
- All WCHF prepared promotional and publicity materials related to FRC reviewed by WRL prior to final distribution.
- Publicize FRC information in WRL newsletter.
- Annual co-sponsorship of FRC workshop and FRC session during the Grantsmanship Center Inc. session (if invited).
- Reprint "pathfinder" rack cards to describe FRC resources.
- Place WCHF PBF bookplates in books.
- Include on WRL web site virtual recognition plaque.
- Include WCHF on PBF plaque on display at the library.

Partnership/Evaluation

- The Partnership Team will work together to develop an annual timetable for implementation, promotion and evaluation.
- Annual evaluation report of project and partnership.
- Commitment to ongoing partnership.

Continued →

Figure 6.3. *(Cont.)*

Partnership Coordination

The WCHF and WRL will designate appropriate staff representation to serve as the partnership team for the coordination of the Funding Research Center. The following staff have been identified as the team, unless otherwise designated and communicated by the partner organization: *WCHF staff:* (Project Manager and WCHF point of contact to and from the Health Foundation), Director, Community Grants Program; Special Projects Director; *WRL Staff:* (Project Manager and WRL point of contact to and from the library), Development Director; Adult Services Department, Collection Development Librarian.

By their signatures below, the representatives of the partner organizations affirm their agreement to the terms and conditions set forth in this document and certify the organization's intent to deliver the services as described.

Williamsburg Community Health Foundation	**Williamsburg Regional Library**
_____	_____
Executive Director	Library Director
Date: _____	Date: _____

Figure 6.4. Williamsburg Regional Library and Williamsburg Community Hospital Cancer Resource Center Agreement

WILLIAMSBURG REGIONAL LIBRARY (WRL) AND WILLIAMSBURG COMMUNITY HOSPITAL (WCH)

CANCER RESOURCE CENTER AGREEMENT

July, 1998

FY1999 GOAL: In partnership, WRL & WCH, with staff assistance from the Williamsburg Community Health Foundation, will plan, establish and market a "self-help" Cancer Resource Center for the community located at the Williamsburg and James City County libraries. The Center will be called the Phillip West Memorial Cancer Resource Center (PWCRC).

LONG RANGE PLAN: Expand the PWCRC to a health information outreach center for the community with long-term funding and trained professional staff.

Continued →

Figure 6.4. (*Cont.*)

PROJECT RESPONSIBILITIES DURING FY1999:

<u>WILLIAMSBURG COMMUNITY HOSPITAL</u>

- $10,000 seed money (Phillip West bequest)

- Needs assessment & evaluation tool

- Marketing of PWCRC to public and area health care providers

- Sponsorship of PWCRC open house(s)

- Programming schedule of cancer-related events at WRL

- Commitment to ongoing partnership

- Continued access to hospital's medical library resources for the public

- Network of physician and medical resources for patron referrals as appropriate

<u>WILLIAMSBURG REGIONAL LIBRARY</u>

- Space at both buildings for PWCRC (enclosed room at JCCL & confidential space at WRL)

- Reference assistance to patrons

- PWCRC Internet web page: design, select links & maintain links

- Project coordinator for CRC startup

- Interlibrary loan service for patron requested books and articles

- Staff training

- Installation and maintenance of computer equipment

Continued →

Figure 6.4. (*Cont.*)

BUDGET NEEDS:

Computers/printers for Internet stations—one for each library	$4,000
Fax machine—one at JCCL for CANCERFAX materials	$500
Project Coordinator —startup of CRC—4 hrs/wk x 52wk @ $17.90/hr*	$4,000
Paper/ink cartridges for fax/Internet subsidy**	$500
Cancer-related books to check out from both libraries***	$750
CANCERFAX (National Cancer Institute) subscription —1 year	$250
TOTAL	$10,000

Notes: * Project Coordinator's hourly rate is based on the FY1998.
** Start-up costs for supplies for one year
*** This amount ($750) will only fund approximately 50 new, lay-oriented cancer-related books for patrons to check out.
 If funding is available, WRL will increase the size of the collection and purchase videos to check out.

PWCRC PROJECT TEAM:
<u>WCH Staff:</u> Community Relations Director; Cancer Services Director; Williamsburg Community Health Foundation Special Projects Director; Medical Librarian; Business Development Director; IS staff
<u>WRL Staff:</u> Adult Services Department, Reference Librarian

WILLIAMSBURG COMMUNITY HOSPITAL

_____

Chief Operating Officer

_____

Date

WILLIAMSBURG REGIONAL LIBRARY

_____

Library Director

_____

Date

Figure 6.5. Williamsburg Regional Library and Williamsburg-James City County Public Schools Partnership Agreement

WILLIAMSBURG REGIONAL LIBRARY (WRL) AND WILLIAMSBURG-JAMES CITY COUNTY PUBLIC SCHOOLS (WJCC)

PARTNERSHIP AGREEMENT FEBRUARY 1, 2003

FOUNDATION A partnership between the Williamsburg Regional Library and the Williamsburg -James City County Public Schools is based on the following principles:

1. The mission statements of WRL and WJCC reflect common purposes to support the educational goals of students and their families; and to work through the community to achieve excellence.

2. Historically the library has been an active participant in enriching area schools' access to children's programming, library collections, student study space, and meeting room space for adult education. Formalizing this relationship acknowledges the value of the library's support. It also creates a strengthened framework that will enable the relationship to grow through system-wide planning and coordination.

3. While the partnership draws on the unique strengths of the two institutions it also benefits from serving the same city-county population.

4. The community is best served by the library and school system working together toward common goals.

GOALS WRL and WJCC will work together as community partners to (a) bring a love of reading and books to area students; (b) teach students to access and analyze information in all formats; and (c) support individuals in their goals for life-long learning.

STRENGTHS
Williamsburg Regional Library: The library offers a tradition of excellence and innovation in collections, services, and programs, serving all area residents. This tradition is due to the knowledge, expertise, and skill of the library staff and strong level of financial support from the City of Williamsburg and James City County.

The library's rich collections include both print and electronic formats, and serve the diverse reading and informational interests of area residents of all ages.

The library's two buildings, the Williamsburg Library and the James City County Library, have been constructed or renovated in the last 6 years. Both facilities are open for service seven days a week. The facilities also serve as a community center, with well-designed meeting room space available for community use. The Bookmobile delivers collections and programming throughout the service area.

Williamsburg-James City County Public Schools: The schools offer excellence in education through well qualified and dedicated staff, and as reflected in the depth of programs available to meet all students' needs. The staff brings unique expertise to the classroom, to school administration, and to specialized resource areas, spanning the range from preschool, Kindergarten through 12th grade, adult basic education (ABE) and English as a second (ESL) language. School staff interact with students on a daily basis. The school division fosters and maintains strong ties to all students and their families creating a strong foundation from which to promote the availability of resources and services in the community.

Continued →

Figure 6.5. *(Cont.)*

WJCC offers well-maintained facilities, which are outfitted with specialized technology learning labs, and theaters. These facilities are located throughout the city and the county with adequate parking.

School staff gather and analyze area demographic information that reflects the changes happening in the community.

INITIATIVES February 1, 2003—June 30, 2004
Resource sharing and program development:

< Continue to offer WRL programs and services to area schools as the budget permits (see attached list of programs available)

< WRL Youth Services, and WJCC District Office and Transportation staff will work together to pilot the Book Buddies Program for selective elementary schools (Matthew Whaley) during National Library Week, April 2003.

< WRL Adult Services and WJCC District Office staff will explore the use of the school's computer labs as future centers for training adults and children to access and analyze information.

< WRL Adult Services and WJCC school media specialists will continue to explore cooperative resource sharing opportunities benefiting both institutions.

Promote library resources and services

< WRL and WJCC will establish a mechanism to promote WRL programs and services to students and their families, and to school employees. WRL will work with the William and Mary Sharpe program to identify the types of marketing pieces that would most effectively promote the library to the school audience. Promotional pieces designed for the school audience will be piloted during 2003-2004.

< Set-up a mechanism and timeline to promote WRL programs and services to school principals and specialized resources departments, including school media specialists, guidance counselors, the Visions program, technology instructors, and ABE/ESL.

< WRL Circulation Department and WJCC will explore the issuance of WRL library cards to all WJCC students, faculty, and staff.

< WJCC and WRL Youth Services will continue to coordinate instructional field trips to the library facilities for the elementary school populations. Instructional field trips will be encouraged for the Bright Beginning program and secondary school students.

Evaluate and document

< WRL, Student Services, and WJCC School Division staff will work together to evaluate the space needs of the ABE/ESL program and the role of the WRL as a space provider. Any agreement to continue using WRL space will be documented and finalized by July 1, 2003.

< WRL and WJCC Division staff will work together to devise an efficient way to evaluate the value and effectiveness of the programs provided by the library to the schools as they relate to the partnership goals.

< WRL and WJCC Division staff will determine criteria for evaluating the success of the library-school partnership.

Continued →

Figure 6.5. (*Cont.*)

WRL will:	WJCC will
Designate appropriate staff to plan, implement, promote, and evaluate the partnership.	Designate appropriate staff to plan, implement, promote, and evaluate the partnership.
Designate appropriate staff to plan, implement, promote, and evaluate the 2003–2004 initiatives, as the budget permits.	Designate appropriate staff to plan, implement, promote, and evaluate the 2003–2004 initiatives, as the budget permits.
Continue to offer supplemental cultural arts and reading-related programs for student audiences.	Assist the library to market its programs and services to WJCC students and their families, faculty, and staff.
Provide meeting facilities for selective WJCC programs.	Provide access to school facilities for selective WRL programs.
Work with WJCC with an ongoing commitment to the partnership.	Work with WRL with an ongoing commitment to the partnership.

FISCAL LIMITATIONS STATEMENT

The next eighteen months will be shaped by significant economic uncertainties affecting WRL, WJCC, area localities, the Commonwealth of Virginia, and the nation as a whole. Although WRL and WJCC are strong institutions, and are committed to accomplishing the initiatives outlined in this letter of agreement, both organizations enter into this agreement with the understanding that budget concerns may limit current or future initiatives.

PARTNERSHIP COORDINATION

The WRL and WJCC will designate appropriate representatives to work as a team to coordinate the overall direction of the partnership, to facilitate joint planning and coordination, and to coordinate the evaluation of the collaborative relationship. Library and school staff delivering programs and services will continue to work directly with one another, guided by the principles and limitations set out in this partnership agreement.

The following people have been identified as the 2003–2004 partnership team: **WJCC**: Supervisor of Instructional Technology and Media. **WRL**: Community Partnership Development Director, Adult Services Director, and, Youth Services Director, and Program Services Director. The Community Partnership Development Director will serve as the library's partnership point person for all communications to and from the library concerning the framework and timeline for the partnership.

Continued →

Figure 6.5. (*Cont.*)

TIMELINE	
January 2003	Approval of the Partnership Agreement by the Superintendent of Schools Approval of Partnership Agreement by the Library Director, Williamsburg Regional Library
February 1, 2003	Implementation of the agreement Begin planning the evaluation component
July 1, 2003	Finalize ABE/ESL program plan for use of WRL facilities
July 1, 2003	Begin evaluating WRL –WJCC initiatives
September 1, 2003	Identify FY 2005 partnership initiatives and budget impact
Spring 2004	Final assessment of FY 2004 initiatives Renewal of the Partnership Agreement for FY 2005

ATTACHMENTS

<   List of WRL—WJCC Cooperative Activities as of January 1, 2003

<   WRL and WJCC mission statements

Williamsburg Regional Library	**Williamsburg-James City County Schools**
(Signature)	_(Signature)_
Library Director	Superintendent of Schools
Date: _____	Date: _____

Continued →

Figure 6.5. *(Cont.)*

Williamsburg Regional Library (WRL)—Williamsburg-James City County Public Schools (WJCC) Cooperative Activities

As of January 1, 2003

GOAL: TO BRING BOOKS AND READING TO AREA YOUTH

Battle of the Books - reading incentive for grades four through eight, based on a specified list of books and a Jeopardy-like competition.

Booked for Breakfast—an early morning story-time for children in the JCC Parks and Recreation Before School program at the elementary schools.

Booked for Lunch—a librarian reads a chapter book with third graders during their lunchtime.

BookSmart—family literacy program for preschool students in the Bright Beginnings program.

Mother Goose Mania—Jeopardy-like competition for third grade students based on nursery rhymes, fairy tales, and picture books.

Spring Fling—theater program held at the Williamsburg Library, usually a puppet show, for preschool children including Bright Beginning students. Usually scheduled in April.

Beacon of Freedom Award—annual children's literature award with a focus on early American history judged by local fourth, fifth, and sixth grade students. WRL, WJCC, and Colonial Williamsburg Foundation sponsor the award.

School visits by WRL Youth Services librarians to promote the library's summer reading program.

School visits with authors/illustrators.

School visits with literary characters such as Clifford the Big Red Dog and Madeline.

Library tours for school classes.

Accelerated Reading lists—maintained for students and parents at both library facilities.

Library Summer Reading Program delivered to all elementary summer school classes.

Summer Reading Lists (middle and high school)—collected and made available to students and parents at both library facilities.

Bookmobile stops- All summer school sites, Recreation Department sites at the schools (set-up with the JCC Parks and Recreation Department), Norge NEED Center, Bight Beginnings.

Youth Services Director serves on Community-School committee.

Continued →

Figure 6.5. (*Cont.*)

GOAL: TO HELP AREA ADULTS REACH THEIR ADULT BASIC EDUCATION OR ENGLISH AS A SECOND LANGUAGE GOALS.

Meeting space is provided by WRL in both library facilities for the ABE, and ESL programs.

GOAL: FACILITATE ACCESS TO RESOURCES FOR ALL STUDENTS TO ACHIEVE LIFE-LONG LEARNING GOALS

List serv—WRL hosts the WJCC School Media Specialist- WRL list serv to electronically share resource news and plan joint staff development programs.

Online full-text databases—WRL and WJCC school media specialists work to promote student home access to the library's many online, full-text databases, such as Gale InfoTrac, Big Chalk, and the Literature and Biography Resource Centers.

Database training for students, faculty, and staff.

Library cards issued to school groups—Since remote access to library databases requires a library card, this effort ensure student access to these as well as all other library resources.

Make library cards available to all WJCC students, faculty and staff to maximize access to all WRL resources.

Online consumer health resources training for summer school health class students (Lafayette and Jamestown high schools).

Fine-free Teacher cards - available to all WJCC classroom and resource teachers (preschool through twelfth grade).

Bibliographies prepared by WRL librarians when requested by teachers.

Student art displays - art teachers bring samples of student work to display in both library facilities.

Back to School Night and other events—WRL librarians attend to promote library's electronic and print resources to students and parents.

Continued →

Figure 6.5. (*Cont.*)

Williamsburg Regional Library
Mission Statement

Free access to information is a foundation of democracy. The Williamsburg Regional Library, a basic government service, provides that access through resources and programs that educate, enrich, entertain, and inform every member of our community.

Vision

In 2005, the residents of Williamsburg, James City County, and Upper York County will recognize that the Williamsburg Regional Library:

- Is the first source for community information needs and a welcoming presence for new arrivals, helping them connect with the community.
- Provides a friendly and informed staff who are vital parts of the cultural, social, and educational life of the community.
- Has a dynamic collection of materials that is regularly evaluated and available in a variety of formats to serve the needs and support the interests of all members of our community.
- Seeks the most appropriate technological innovations while maintaining a strong commitment to traditional library services.
- Extends services beyond its walls, seeking out increasing access points for information, collections, and programs.
- Provides early language experiences for all children in the community.
- Teaches community members how to gather, evaluate, and use information.
- Creates partnerships with civic organizations, educational and government entities, businesses, and libraries to reach new user groups and expand access to library services.
- Is a community center that encourages and supports interaction among all our residents.
- Is a responsible steward of its available resources.

Core Values

WE VALUE FREE AND CONFIDENTIAL ACCESS TO INFORMATION

Open and unrestricted access to information from all library resources will be available and, when possible, in multiple formats to meet the individual needs of all residents of Williamsburg, James City County, and Upper York County. Access will be convenient and confidential. Williamsburg Regional Library supports freedom of speech and the right of residents to select the information appropriate for their needs.

WE VALUE ALL RESIDENTS IN OUR COMMUNITY

Each individual in our community will receive the best library service possible. Everyone will be treated with respect and will receive friendly, courteous service.

Continued →

Figure 6.5. (*Cont.*)

WE VALUE A LITERATE COMMUNITY

Literacy is important to the successful functioning of a democratic society. Williamsburg Regional Library provides a lifelong ladder of literacy through programs, services, collections, and cooperative ventures with community partners.

WE VALUE STRENGTH FOUND IN DIVERSITY

Our resources, like our residents, form a tapestry embracing multiple cultures, values, and lifestyles. Discovering and sharing our experiences through materials, programs, and interactions enriches us all.

WE VALUE OUR STAFF

Access to information demands the skills of a talented, well-trained, and knowledgeable staff. Williamsburg Regional Library provides a positive work environment that respects each staff member's unique contributions.

WE VALUE ETHICAL, FISCALLY RESPONSIBLE STEWARDSHIP OF PUBLIC RESOURCES

Each employee of the Williamsburg Regional Library is a steward of the public trust. All staff exercise prudence when using and/or allocating any library funds or resources. Staff work with other community partners when possible to best utilize all resources.

7

Evaluating Partnerships

One of the most difficult steps encountered in any sort of program or service is the evaluation. It is also one of the most important aspects of ensuring both that the service or program is meeting the needs of the institution and its users and that the use of time and resources on the program is justified. As libraries find themselves increasingly short of funds, making the case to funding bodies that the institution is acting in a fiscally responsible fashion becomes vital. Being able to show positive results also makes it easier to ask for increased funding to support successful programs and services. For these reasons, spending time planning how to evaluate the library's partnering program is essential.

When evaluating partnership efforts in the library, there are two factors to consider. Both help you build a successful picture of how the partnership is operating, and they should be looked at in tandem.

The first is the evaluation of the entire partnership. You need to evaluate the overall partnership on a regular basis, and the time frame for the evaluation should be clarified in the partnership letter of agreement. You should plan on evaluating each partnership annually, though there may be specific relationships that can be evaluated less frequently. Initially, it may be useful to both parties to do a six-month evaluation of a new relationship. This is especially true if there are concerns about how the two partners match up. On the other hand, ongoing relationships where a level of trust has been established may only need to be formally evaluated every other year. The frequency of evaluation depends to a large extent on the need of the library or of the community partner to document the success of the project.

In the overall partnership evaluation, both partners should look carefully at their relationship and try to answer the following questions:

Is the partnership working?,

How are the communication mechanisms functioning?, and, most important

Is the relationship a good match for both partners?

This evaluation element focuses on process. The purpose is to establish whether the two partners are working well together and to ensure that the overall aims of the partnership are still being met (from both parties' perspective).

The evaluation of the overall partnership effort brings the partners together for an annual relationship checkup. This is the time to examine where the partnership has been and review where both sides see the relationship going. The partners can raise concerns and look at new issues that may need to be addressed as the organizations change or as missions evolve. Later in this chapter we discuss the actual mechanics of evaluating the partnership as a whole and include examples of the evaluation tools that we use.

The second evaluative element that needs to be considered is the assessment of the specific initiatives that are part of each partnership effort. These initiatives do need to be evaluated regularly for each partnering cycle. There are a number of questions that you need to ask as you evaluate the partnership initiatives each year:

- Were the specific initiatives accomplished?

- If some were not accomplished, why not?

- Were the initiatives useful to the partnership?

- In light of the reasons for partnering (reaching new users, reaching current users in a new way, tapping into community assets and strengths, gaining support for library resources or programs, gaining community feedback, and creating new resources), can you show that the initiatives supported one or more of the reasons?

When you are evaluating the projects related to a partnership, it is useful to devise tools to gather statistical data to indicate their success. For example, if your goal is to reach new users through a particular program, you should show that you did indeed do so. For example, the Williamsburg Regional Library uses program evaluation forms that ask attendees at partnership-related programs a variety of questions (see figure 7.1 for an example of the form). Using this form, we were able to document that over one year of programming related to the Phillip West Memorial Cancer Resource Center, developed in partnership with the Sentara Williamsburg Community Hospital, 84 percent of program attendees already had library cards. Once you have the data collected, then you need to decide if 16 percent non-card holder attendance over the course of the year supports the goal of reaching new users.

Figure 7.1. Program and Library Service Evaluation Form

Program and Library Service Evaluation

Program name: _____

Date: _____

Your opinion is important to us. Please help us improve both the Library's programs and services by giving us your feedback.

1. The information presented met my expectations for program content.
   (4) Strongly Agree   (3) Agree   (2) Disagree (1) Strongly Disagree

2. The material presented was easily understood.
   (4) Strongly Agree   (3) Agree   (2) Disagree (1) Strongly Disagree

3. I could hear the presenters clearly.
   (4) Strongly Agree   (3) Agree   (2) Disagree (1) Strongly Disagree

4. This program has added to my understanding of this topic.
   (4) Strongly Agree   (3) Agree   (2) Disagree (1) Strongly Disagree

5. Have you ever been in one of the library facilities before today? Check all that apply
   Williamsburg Library
   James City County Library
   Bookmobile
   this is my first visit

6. How often do you visit the library facilities?
   weekly
   monthly
   other_____

7. Do you have a library card?
   yes
   no

Your opinion matters, please continue to answer the questions on the back!

Figure 7.1. (*Cont.*)

8. What library resources do you use? (Check all that apply)
   adult books and printed materials
   adult programs and concerts
   children's books and printed materials
   children's programs and concerts
   computers
   help from a librarian
   meeting space
   reference services
   tax forms
   videos/dvds/audiobooks
   other_____

9. How did you hear about this program? Check all that apply.
   library's newsletter
   flyer/poster
   newspaper paid ad (which newspaper?) _____
   newspaper article (which newspaper?) _____
   library's electronic mail list
   friend/relative
   other _____

10. How long have you lived in the community?
    less than one year
    1 to 5 years
    6 to 10 years
    over 11 years
    visitor

11. What is your racial background?
    African American
    Asian
    Hispanic
    White (Caucasian)
    other

12. Which age group do you belong to?
    0–5
    6–15
    16–30
    31–65
    66+

Similarly, if you are developing a partnership that aims to develop new resources, you should be able to put together hard data on the value of the resource:

- Was money saved by working jointly to develop the resource?

- Can you document use of the new resource?

    - Web site hits

    - Circulation of materials in a new collection

    - Patron use numbers for research tools

- Did the creation of the new resource save staff time (and thus money)?

Another important reason to regularly evaluate your partnership initiatives is to ensure that the relationship still holds up for the reasons you intended. Sometimes, a particular initiative is still useful to a partnership, and you will want to continue pursuing it in the coming year, perhaps with a shifted emphasis.

As an example, imagine that your library develops a partnership with local recreation centers with the goal of reaching minority users. You began a partnership initiative to reach and recruit new library users, with library staff going to the center once every month to offer library cards. After a certain point, the library will have reached all of the potential new users that it can through this initiative. This does not mean that you need to stop the outreach associated with this partnership, but you need to look at what other possibilities this initiative affords. Perhaps it is a good time to begin to promote new library services and resources through this partner, or perhaps the partnership can be focused on developing support for the library. In all cases, the regular assessment of partnership initiatives allows both the library and the community partner the opportunity to shape the partnership so that it more fully realizes the needs of both institutions.

Libraries with a wide range of partnerships will find that these relationships vary in terms of the number and scope of the partnership initiatives. Smaller partnerships may only have a single initiative, while larger partnerships may have numerous pieces, reaching across several departments. The Williamsburg Regional Library's partnership with the Williamsburg-James City County Public Schools has multiple initiatives, involving four different library departments. When working on a large partnership, it is not necessary to evaluate all of the initiatives right away. It is important though to decide upfront what you do want to evaluate over the course of the year. Both institutions need to decide on which pieces of the partnership to evaluate when, and you also need to agree at this point on a method of evaluation.

Evaluation of partnership initiatives is not just busy work. It is one of the most important tools that you have for justifying to the library director, the library board, and your partners that the relationship is useful and worthy of support. You will find partnership evaluation much simpler if you do not front-load a new partnership with lots of projects the first year. In developing initiatives for a new relationship, first pick ones that you can evaluate and that will give you valuable information about the relationship. Later on, you can add new initiatives and expand the reach of the partnership.

Overall, the evaluation part of the partnership process helps your library and your community partner determine whether the concept of partnering is working as a tool for both institutions. There may also be circumstances under which the evaluation process brings to light concerns that were not immediately evident in setting up the partnership. It is certainly possible to have a partnering relationship that runs very smoothly, where communication is flawless, and whose initiatives all come off without a hitch, but that does not really support the mission of the library.

The evaluation process asks the partnership manager to look back at the six reasons that the library develops partnerships and to determine that the current relationship is still meeting at least one of those needs. If not, even if the partnership functions smoothly, you need to look at why you are spending time and resources on it. It may be that there are political reasons to continue the relationship. Perhaps a local funding body views this relationship in a positive manner, and to end the relationship would be costly in terms of political capital. But it is also possible that the relationship needs to be modified or even ended. A careful evaluation will make this sort of decision easier.

By using the six reasons for partnering as the basis for developing a thoughtful evaluation of a community partnership, the library can also catch those relationships where the partnership is fruitful for the library staff person managing it but perhaps not for the library as a whole. Again, in a case of this sort the evaluation portion clarifies whether the relationship is a good match for the library, regardless of its positive effect on the individuals involved. When you are trying to prioritize partnerships, it is essential to consider the value of the relationship to the entire library, not simply to an individual department or staff person.

Doing the Evaluation

By simplifying the evaluation process, you increase the likelihood that staff will complete the evaluations in a timely fashion, and that you will get useful information from the evaluation. Nonetheless, it is important to remember that, like most processes that involve working with another institution, performing the partnership evaluation takes time. Make sure that you build in sufficient time to get the partnership evaluation done before a new partnering cycle begins. For instance, the Williamsburg Regional Library partners with the local AARP to provide tax assistance to seniors and low-income community members. This particular partnership is most active from December through May. The partnership evaluation for this relationship takes place in June, just following tax season. This allows us to most effectively address problems, and to plan initiatives to meet new challenges, while these needs are clear in the minds of both organizations. Make sure to build a deadline for evaluation into your partnership agreement.

In some ways the evaluation process we use is similar to the process of drafting a letter of agreement, discussed in chapter 5. The partnership manager fills out an evaluation form. The community partnership development director provides assistance and direction and reviews the completed forms with the library's partner manager. There is a section of the evaluation form for the community partner's partnership manager to fill out. After review, forms are exchanged, and the two parties meet to discuss any concerns that have arisen from the evaluation process and to plan out new initiatives for the coming partnership year. The community partnership development director shares the completed evaluation with the library director at the time of the renewal of the partnership letter of agreement. (See figure 7.2.)

Figure 7.2. Evaluating Library Partnerships

EVALUATING LIBRARY PARTNERSHIPS

Attached is a partnership evaluation form for use by both the library partnership coordinator and the partnering agency partnership coordinator. Most questions consist of three parts: a question about achieving one of the specific goals that partnering is intended to satisfy per the library's strategic plan; a section to rate the importance of that goal for this particular partnership; and a section for elaborating on how and why the goal was realized. Part I of the evaluation is for library staff. Part II is for partnering agencies. For assistance in completing this evaluation and other related questions please contact the Williamsburg Regional Library Community Partnership Development Director.

Below are some project measurement tools that should be considered in preparing this evaluation.

GOAL 1. Reach new users

survey	new user registrations	program evaluation form	interviews or focus groups	program attendance figures	

GOAL 2. Reach library users in a new way

survey	number of circulations	program evaluation form	interviews or focus groups	program attendance figures	

GOAL 3. Tap into community assets and strengths

List of, and $ value of assets/ strengths	program attendance figures	survey	interviews or focus groups		

GOAL 4. Gain support for library resources/programs

survey	program attendance figures	new user registrations	number of circulations	monetary contribution	

GOAL 5. Gain valuable feedback

survey	interviews or focus groups	program attendance figures	program evaluation form		

GOAL 6. Create new resources

monetary contribution	number of circulations	website hits	lists of created resources		

Continued →

Figure 7.2. (*Cont.*)

WRL Partnership Evaluation Form

Project Manager:
WRL Department:
Other WRL departments involved with this partnership:

Community partner:
Project Explanation:

Evaluation of Partnership for the year:

Date evaluation completed:

SECTION I: LIBRARY PARTNERSHIP COORDINATOR

1. Did the partnership reach new users?
___ Definitely ___ Somewhat ___ No ___ Not Sure

On a scale of 1 to 10 (with 10 being most important) please rate the importance of reaching new users for this partnership project:

   1   2   3   4   5   6   7   8   9   10

Estimate how many new users were reached and explain how you know they were reached (attach measurement tool results):

2. Did the partnership project reach library patrons in a new way?
___ Definitely ___ Somewhat ___ No ___ Not Sure

On a scale of 1 to 10 (with 10 being most important) please rate the importance of reaching library patrons in a new way for this partnership:

   1   2   3   4   5   6   7   8   9   10

Explain the new way in which patrons were reached and how you know they were reached (attach measurement tool results):

3. Did the partnership tap into community assets and strengths?
___ Definitely ___ Somewhat ___ No ___ Not Sure

On a scale of 1 to 10 (with 10 being most important) please rate the importance of tapping into community assets and strengths for this partnership:

   1   2   3   4   5   6   7   8   9   10

What is the value to the library?

Continued →

Figure 7.2. (*Cont.*)

4. Did the partnership gain support for library resources/programs?
____ Definitely ____ Somewhat ____ No ____ Not Sure

On a scale of 1 to 10 (with 10 being most important) please rate the importance of gaining support for library resources/programs for this partnership:

   1   2   3   4   5   6   7   8   9   10

Explain the support gained for library resources/programs and how you measured the support:

5. Did the partnership enable the library to gain valuable community feedback?
____ Definitely ____ Somewhat ____ No ____ Not Sure

On a scale of 1 to 10 (with 10 being most important) please rate the importance of gaining community feedback for this partnership:

   1   2   3   4   5   6   7   8   9   10

Describe feedback collection methods, forums and other pertinent details:

6. Did the partnership create new library resources?
____ Definitely ____ Somewhat ____ No ____ Not Sure

On a scale of 1 to 10 (with 10 being most important) please rate the importance of creating new Library resources for this partnership:

   1   2   3   4   5   6   7   8   9   10

List what resources were created:

Could the library have created this resource without forming this partnership? Explain your answer:

7. Were requirements of the Letter of Agreement satisfied? If no, explain below.
____ Definitely ____ Somewhat ____ No ____ Not Sure

Explain elements that were not satisfied, why and how this affected the partnership:

Continued →

Figure 7.2. (*Cont.*)

8. What library resources were used to support this partnership?

9. What effect did this partnership project have on other WRL departments?

10. What changes do you recommend to the partnership/project?

11. How has this partnership contributed to the library's vision of 2005? How does it fit with the library's strategic plan and your department's implementation plan?

Continued →

Figure 7.2. *(Cont.)*

SECTION II: PARTNERING AGENCY PARTNERSHIP COORDINATOR

1. Did the partnership with the Library meet your organization's expectations and goals?

____ Definitely ____ Somewhat ____ No ____ Not Sure

Explain expectations and goals that were both met and unmet:

2. Were requirements of the Letter of Agreement satisfied?, If no, explain below.

____ Definitely ____ Somewhat ____ No ____ Not Sure

Explain elements that were not satisfied, why and how this affected the partnership:

3. What changes do you recommend to the partnership/project with the library?

By signing you certify that you have reviewed the entire evaluation and completed all sections appropriate to your organization.

_____   _____
Library Partnership Coordinator   Partnering Agency Partnership
                                           Coordinator

The partnership evaluation form is tied to the broad partnership process, not to any one initiative. The form uses the same questions that are asked in the proposal stage of partnership development that relate directly to the reasons for partnering.

- Did the partnership reach new users?

- Did the partnership project reach library patrons in a new way?

- Did the partnership tap into community assets and strengths?

- Did the partnership gain support for library resources/programs?

- Did the partnership enable the library to gain valuable community feedback?

- Did the partnership create new library resources?

In addition, the form asks other questions that relate to the specific initiatives and goals of the partnership, as well as asking about future plans:

- Were requirements of the letter of agreement satisfied?

- What effect did this partnership project have on other library departments?

- What changes do you recommend to the partnership/project?

- How does it fit with the library's strategic plan and your department's implementation plan?

- How has this partnership contributed to the library's vision?

Most questions consist of three parts: a question about achieving one of the specific goals that partnering is intended to satisfy per the library's strategic plan, a section to rate the importance of that goal for this particular partnership, and a section for elaborating on how and why the goal was realized. As the partnership manager answers these questions, it should become clear how well the partnership fulfilled its purpose of supporting the library's mission. This, in turn, will enable the partnership manager to work with the community partner in developing the goals and outcomes for the next year.

As mentioned before, most partnerships work across at least two library departments, and sometimes more. Because of the cross-departmental nature of most relationships with community partners, it is valuable to have a question on the partnership evaluation form that requires the library's partnership manager to look at how this particular partnership affects other areas of the library. As the two partnership managers meet to discuss new initiatives and goals, the library's representative must be aware of the implications of any new projects for others in the library and must seek support and commitment from those departments that will be affected.

As a part of the evaluation form, we include a table that lists project measurement tools that can be used to determine whether the partnership is effectively meeting one or more of the six reasons to partner. Each of the different goals of partnering has a set of mechanisms that can be used to evaluate its success. Listing these tools on the evaluation form makes it easier for the partnership manager(s) to plan ahead how best to track and assess the partnership. The project goals and potential measurement tools are listed in figure 7.3.

Figure 7.3. Partnership Goals

GOAL 1. Reach new users • survey • new user registrations • program evaluation form • interviews or focus groups • program attendance figures	GOAL 2. Reach library users in a new way • survey • number of circulations • program evaluation form • interviews or focus groups • program attendance figures
GOAL 3. Tap into community assets and strengths • List of, and $ value of assets/strengths • program attendance figures • survey • interviews or focus groups	GOAL 4. Gain support for library resources/programs • survey • program attendance figures • new user registrations • number of circulations • monetary contribution
GOAL 5. Gain valuable feedback • survey • interviews or focus groups • program attendance figures • program evaluation form	GOAL 6. Create new resources • monetary contribution • number of circulations • website hits • lists of created resources

One question that often arises in partnership evaluation is how to determine the best time to evaluate an ongoing relationship. As mentioned above, it is not necessary to have all partnerships in the library on the same evaluation cycle, and from a staff workload perspective it works best to have staggered evaluations. In setting up the time period to evaluate, keep in mind the library's institutional cycles. If you feel that a particular partnership is going to frequently require funding that needs to be included in the library budget, you will want to make sure that the evaluation function is done well in advance of when budget requests are due. Similarly, if a partnership has initiatives that are limited to a specific time of year, make sure that the evaluation process follows as close as possible on the conclusion of these initiatives, allowing you to assess and plan for the coming year well in advance.

Remember that most partnerships take time to become established. You probably will not be able to get a comprehensive evaluation of the partnership within the fiscal year in which the relationship was established. This should not be a problem, as any formal partnership that has reached the marriage stage should have already been either tested out during the engagement or be a formalization of a long-term but unformalized relationship. Because of the ongoing nature of the partnership process, it is vital to keep members of the library board informed about the evaluation process. As part of the preprocess of educating boards about partnerships, you should make them aware that partnership commitments extend beyond a single year. Reporting to the library board on partnering-related topics and giving them copies of important documents (especially letters of agreement) not only keeps them informed about partnering but also gives them a better understanding about how the process works.

Partnership Program Evaluation

We have also developed a form to use in assessing individual programs that are part of the partnering agreement. Data gathered from these initiatives can be useful to both the library and the community partner, not only in evaluating the overall success of the partnership, but also in examining how the library is serving particular constituencies.

For any partnership that has a programming element, we select some or all of the events to evaluate. In addition to questions that address the specific program, there are certain core data elements that the program and library service evaluation form tries to capture (see figure 7.1, pages 103–4, for sample form). These elements allow the library to look for trends and patterns in how the community is using the services and programs offered by the library. The information that you gather here should help your library develop a clearer "community portrait," making it easier to improve existing services and procedures or to develop new ones as necessary.

We have obtained some very useful information from the answers that program attendees gave to these questions. For instance, we discovered that a majority of people who attend library programs have found out about the event through the local newspaper. This discovery has led the library to increase its efforts at promoting library services and events through the newspaper. It has also caused us to examine the value of paid advertising in the paper. As we plan new events and services, library staff commonly build advertising costs into the budget. A revision of the library newsletter to make it a more effective tool in terms of promoting services and programs also resulted, in part, from information gathered as part of the partnership program evaluations.

When you create forms to use for partnership program and library service evaluation, try to keep them as short as possible. The longer a form is, the fewer people will fill it out, and the more difficult it is to process. Our goal is to keep the program evaluation form to no more than two sides of a single letter sheet. A goal in developing the program evaluation form should be to create an instrument that can be adapted to a variety of programs across the various library partnerships. When you are developing the form, think about what sort of information is most useful for the library to collect. Do you need to know where people live who are coming to the library programs in order to target specific parts of the community? Do you want to know education levels of program attendees? If so, ask these questions, but try to keep the form a easy as possible to fill out.

Also, remember that the questions on the form are not set in stone. Be flexible as you develop the form, and try to create one that can be customized to meet the needs of a particular library department or partner. The basic form should be general enough to work well in most situations, but for some programs or audiences, you may wish to modify your questions to generate information that will be useful to the library or to the community partner.

Points to Remember about Partnership Evaluation

For most libraries, partnering is a new tool. Because of this you need to watch closely to see if it is meeting the needs of the organization. Initially, there will be excitement about the possibilities that are offered by developing relationships with organizations in the community. It is important to temper this excitement with the understanding that partnering requires a commitment of staff time and library resources to succeed. If the library will not or cannot shift resources to partnering and make it a strategic tool for achieving the library's mission, partnering efforts will have a difficult time succeeding. By using the evaluation tools and processes discussed in this chapter, you will be able to make careful decisions about which partnerships are working and which are not. Knowing this sort of information allows the library administration to prioritize partnership opportunities based on something more than a vague feel about what is or is not working.

Partnering and Outcome-Based Evaluation

One of the hottest topics in library program evaluation right now is outcome-based evaluation. It is seen as an increasingly important tool for local governments and nonprofits to assess the value of what they do, not simply by looking at the output measures but by trying to establish what impact the program or service has had by looking at "the achievements or changes in skill, knowledge, attitude, behavior, condition, or life status for program participants."[1] A useful introduction to outcome-based evaluation for libraries, created as a joint project of the School of Information at University of Michigan and the Information School at the University of Washington, can be found at http://www.si.umich.edu/libhelp/toolkit/index.html. You may find that state libraries, funding bodies, potential community partners, or other organizations will be pushing for the library to use outcome-based evaluations as part of the ongoing assessment of library programs and services, including partnership development.

Applying outcome evaluations to partnerships can be difficult. Remember that the partnership evaluation is looking to assess the "process" piece; that is, you are evaluating whether this particular partnership is effective as a tool or method of supporting the library's mission and vision. Partnerships operate at the institutional level, working through community gatekeepers, not at the grassroots level of reaching out to individuals. As a result, it is hard to use outcome-based evaluation to establish the impact of a partnership on a particular group of people. Evaluating the overall partnership involves making decisions about whether this relationship allowed the library to further its reach into the community.

You can, however, use the tools of outcome-based evaluation to assess the impact of specific partnership initiatives. Here, the program or service is aimed at addressing the needs of a specific user population, and there may be ways that you can incorporate outcome-based evaluation into these plans. Again, do not try to apply outcome evaluation to all of the initiatives associated with a particular partnership or to all of your partnerships. Select a few initiatives that lend themselves to outcome-based assessment. For example, the Williamsburg Regional Library's partnership with the Williamsburg-James City County Public Schools involves improving reading skills of local students. Currently, the schools measure student reading levels in schools as part of their own assessment process. Through the partnership, we are working to assess our joint efforts at promoting reading in one or two of the schools by looking at the improvement in reading level of students who participate in these programs. This is an instance where outcome-based evaluation can be usefully applied within a partnership.

Note

1. Joan C. Durrance, and Karen Fisher, *How Libraries and Librarians Help: Outcome-Based Evaluation Toolkit,* available at http://www.si.umich.edu/libhelp/toolkit/index.html (accessed November 4, 2003).

8

Partnership Management

One of the most exciting aspects of creating a successful partnership program in the library is the opportunity for all staff to become involved in the process. As discussed in previous chapters, ideas for potential partnerships can arise from any level in the organization. This openness to broad participation in the process creates a level of staff enthusiasm about and support of the partnering process that is key to making partnering work.

In addition to coming up with ideas for potential partnerships, staff at all levels may also find themselves managing these partnerships. As in any situation, there are times when partnership management needs to come from the upper levels of library administration. More complex partnerships that affect several library departments may need to be coordinated at a higher level. Nonetheless, even these larger partnerships often have specific initiatives that can be managed by other library staff.

There are risks involved in allowing staff the freedom to work with a community partner. The partnership managers are the library's representatives in the community (at least in the portion of the community where they are working), and it is essential that the interaction between the library and the community partner be a positive one. A badly managed partnership results in the loss of community goodwill, in addition to being a waste of library time and resources.

For some institutions, it may require some loosening of control or flattening of hierarchical structures to allow staff from throughout the institution the opportunity to implement partnering ideas that they have put forth. This sort of openness can lead to development of a stronger library. Staff have the opportunity develop skills as they are faced with new situations; new leaders are discovered who might have otherwise been overlooked; and increased responsibilities for partnership management, when carried out carefully and well, can result in rewards for staff, in terms of both recognition and remuneration.

Skill Set for a Partnership Manager

Every partnership that the library develops will be different and will require the partnership manager to have strengths in one of a variety of areas. That being said, it is possible to outline the skills necessary for managing a partnership. As you go through these, it will probably become clear, as it did for us, that these skills are really no different than those that you would look for in any well-qualified staff member.

Communication

It is absolutely crucial that a partnership manager have outstanding communication skills. In each partnership, the library staff person who is managing the partnership creates the image that the community partner will have of the library. The partnership manager is the person who is responsible for building the trust relationship that is at the core of any successful partnership. Developing that trust means working closely with a community partner and necessitates that both managers keep each other informed about what is going on in their organization and what issues may be arising. At the same time, the library's partnership manager needs to excel at keeping library staff and administration informed about what is going on with their partnership. This is especially important in partnering situations that involve more than one library department. The library's partnership manager should know when to bring other library staff into the discussion. If the partnership manager makes promises that require support from other departments but has not communicated with those departments in advance to get them on board, the partnership will quickly get bogged down.

In addition to being able to communicate clearly, both in writing and orally, a partnership manager must be open to confronting problems and issues that develop. Librarians are no different from other people in wanting to avoid confrontation whenever possible. In developing a mutually trusting relationship, however, the partners both have to be willing to communicate problems that have arisen, and they must be willing to work together to solve them. We have found that most problems that arise with partners develop because of unclear communication of needs and expectations. Failure to let the partner know when these situations arise often leads to small issues becoming larger difficulties.

The Big Picture

As well as being a strong communicator, a successful partnership manager needs to take a broad view of the library and the community. For a partnership to flourish, the manager must be alert to new opportunities within the relationship. Partnerships are most successful when the library's partnership manager has the ability to see the community partner's perspective and needs even before the partner is aware of these. Having a clear understanding of the local community—knowing who the community gatekeepers are, where the community is heading as a whole, who the movers and shakers are—enables the partnership manager to regularly reassess the partnership and be responsive to changes in the partner's situation and in the community as a whole. In addition, the manager must be aware of changes within the library and recognize how these changes offer both opportunities and challenges.

Library staff members who are managing partnerships must be alert to situations and issues in a librarywide fashion and cannot be focused on the aims and goals of their own department. In seeking out partnership managers, look for individuals who have a strong grasp of the library's mission and vision and seek to place the role of their department within this broader vision. Without this comprehensive understanding of the library's mission, it will be difficult for the prospective partnership manager to have a sense of how the library's and the partner's missions match up.

Organizational Skills

A successful partnership manager must also have excellent project management skills. Managing a partnership requires the ability to set agendas, meet deadlines, organize and carry out initiatives, and carefully monitor and evaluate the ongoing relationship. While these are skills that an administrator looks for in any staff, they are essential skills for a partnership manager. Again, the community partner will be looking to the library's partnership manager not only as its main contact but also as the representative of the library as an institution. Poor project management will reflect badly not only on the individual but also on the library.

Leadership

Staff who are partnership managers should be seen as leaders in the library. This does not mean that they have to be in positions of authority in the institution. What it does mean is that they have to be people who can generate excitement among staff about the possibilities that their particular partnership provides. These will be staff members who have a focus on or interest in things beyond their own department, who will set high expectations for the partnering relationship and strive to carry them out, and who will be champions for the relationship within the institution and with the community partner. In many, if not all, partnerships, the library will be the leading partner and the driving force behind the relationship. The library's partnership manager's enthusiasm and passion for the project will be crucial to its success.

Objectivity

At the same time, it is important that a partnership manager not let his or her ego get in the way of assessing the partnership. Specific community partnerships quickly come to be identified with their library managers. The partnership manager develops name recognition both inside the library and in the community. While there is nothing wrong with this identification per se, be careful that passion for and identification with a particular partnership does not keep the manager from making objective assessments of the relationship. The partnership manager must be able to say when the relationship or initiatives are not working, as well as basking in the reflected glow of a successful community partnership.

Endurance

Finally, a partnership manager must be patient. As mentioned before, community partnership development is a slow process. The manager must accept the need for documentation and evaluation and must be willing to work within the process and accept bureaucratic procedures. Staff who are passionate about an idea, but who cannot see the value of the process to partnering, are not going to be good representatives of the library within the community.

To sum up, following are the basic qualities of the successful partnership manager:

- Is a strong communicator both up and down the library hierarchy

- Has the ability to build trust-based relationships

- Has a broad view of the library's mission and vision and the community it serves

- Is responsive to change

- Is a strong project manager

- Leads from where he or she is in the organization

- Has a passion and excitement for partnering

- Can remain objective about their projects

- Has patience

- Takes a proactive approach to the partnership by anticipating potential problems or issues

Training Staff for Partnership Management

Developing successful partnership managers begins with the hiring process. Library staff who are responsible for hiring should keep in mind the possibility that all new employees come into the library as potential partnership managers. As you make hiring decisions, look for the qualities mentioned previously. Once you have hired a staff person, be sure to include a presentation on partnering as part of your orientation process.

When preparing existing staff to manage partnerships, lay a foundation that builds both an understanding of and an excitement about the partnering process. Some of the tactics for building this foundation are discussed in earlier chapters. These include making staff a part of the library's planning process, including staff in the development of the library's assets and strengths list, and making partnering information readily available to all staff via a partnering Web site. Other methods for building staff knowledge of partnering include making sure to announce new partnerships to all library staff and celebrating new "marriages" in some way. The community partnership development director should also make periodic presentations to the various library departments to keep them apprised of what is going on with partnering endeavors and to demonstrate how to go about developing a partnership.

The first steps to developing good partnership managers in the library come through good hiring decisions and building an understanding of the importance of partnering among all staff. Keeping the process inclusive and transparent reinforces to library staff that they are considered an important part of the process, both in terms of idea generation and as potential partnership managers.

The next training step comes when a staff member comes up with a feasible idea for a formal partnership, either a marriage or an engagement. If this staff person is interested in coordinating the partnership (assuming it is approved), there should be some specific training on how to manage a community partnership. Much of this training will be done by the community partnership development director, who has the best understanding of the partnering process and should be the most effective person to train new partnership managers in how to draft a partnership agreement and then how to make sure that the goals of that agreement are achieved. There are several aspects of this formal training for new partnership managers.

First, any new partnership manager must have a very clear understanding of the library's mission and vision and be able to articulate these to the community partner. Without this basic understanding, the new manager will not have a sense of how to match the library's mission with that of the community partner, making it difficult to explain why this is a valuable partnership to the library, and making it impossible to draft a useful letter of agreement. It is important for any new partnership manager to remember that the community partner will view him or her not as a representative of a particular library department but as the representative of the entire library. Thus, the new partnership manager must be very clear about what the library can and cannot offer as part of the partnership. Again, this awareness arises from an understanding of the library's resources and how they can be used.

Often, staff who are not part of the library administration may not have a strong sense of this factor, and it is important that the library's community partnership development director work with new managers to ensure that they are not promising things that the library will not be able to deliver, such as meeting room space, staff time, and financial support. Often this lack of understanding reveals itself in the new partnership manager making promises or laying out plans that involve another department without first speaking with the head of that department. It is easy to get caught up in the excitement of possibilities.

Part of the training for new partnership managers is to be learn to temper this excitement with the reality of what can be done. The internal review process for developing partnerships should help eliminate problems before they occur.

This ties in with the second part of the formal training for new partnership managers in the library, that is, the development of a clear understanding of the internal policies and procedures related to partnership development. As discussed in chapter 4, one of the reasons for setting up an internal structure for partnering is to lend consistency to the efforts. It is essential for new partnership managers to not only understand what the structure is but also commit to working within that structure. This is an area where we have found that the development of a partnership development Web site has proven invaluable.

Prospective partnership managers can use the information on this site (see details in chapter 3) to build their understanding of how the library does partnering. The FAQs detail many of the questions about day-to-day processes that arise as the new partnership manager begins working with a community partner (see box).

Frequently Asked Questions for Williamsburg Regional Library Partnership Managers

Williamsburg Regional Library Questions

1. What is the Mission Statement of the Williamsburg Regional Library?

   Free access to information is a foundation of democracy. The Williamsburg Regional Library, a basic government service, provides that access through resources and programs that educate, enrich, entertain and inform every member of our community.

2. What are the goals of the Williamsburg Regional Library regarding community partnerships?

   As our Vision Statement for 2005 states, the Williamsburg Regional Library has creative partnerships with civic organizations, businesses, libraries, and educational and government entities to reach new user groups and expand access to library services. The Williamsburg Regional Library is one of the few libraries in the nation that administers a formal program to develop community partnerships.

3. How does a partnership with the Williamsburg Regional Library benefit an organization?

   Partnerships with the Williamsburg Regional Library are designed to be mutually beneficial to each of the parties involved. A partnership with the library can provide positive publicity for an organization with the local community, as well as provide access to resources and services.

4. How are the partnership policies of the Williamsburg Regional Library overseen?

   The Williamsburg Regional Library has a Community Partnership Development Group (CPDG) whose membership includes the library director and selected representatives of the library's management ensemble team (MEMS). It was established to facilitate a strategic and integrated approach to partnering with civic organizations, educational and government entities, businesses, and libraries to reach new user groups, to expand access to library services, and to further shared library-community goals.

5. How many partnerships does the Williamsburg Regional Library currently manage?

The Williamsburg Regional Library currently manages partnership agreements with over fifteen organizations.

6. With who does the Williamsburg Regional Library currently partner?

For information on current partnerships with the Williamsburg Regional Library, refer to the WRL Web site for further details: http://www.wrl.org/.

Partnership Process Questions

1. What are the different levels of partnership that the library offers?

Glance: any overture or contact between the library and a community group, organization, business, school, or government agency. Glances may be in the form of written communications (including letters and e-mail), a visit, a telephone call, or participation in a group, club, or association as a library representative.

Date: an agreement between the library and a community partner to accomplish a specific, short- term activity or commitment.

Engagement: a formal agreement between the library and a community partner to work together toward a marriage after an experimental phase.

Marriage: a formal agreement between the library and a community partner with compatible goals to share the work, risk, and the results or proceeds. The library and the community partner jointly invest in resources, experience mutual benefits, and share risk, responsibility, authority, and accountability. Marriages form for long-term benefits to the partners.

2. How are the various levels of partnership formalized?

Glance: not formalized by a written letter of agreement—these commitments can be confirmed either orally or by letter.

Date: not formalized by a written letter of agreement—these commitments can be confirmed either orally or by letter.

Engagement: formalized by a written letter of agreement with the purpose of working toward a marriage, if possible.

Marriage: formalized by a written letter of agreement with the purpose of fostering a long-term, mutually beneficial relationship.

3. How long are the partnership agreements generally signed for?

Partnership agreements usually are signed for one year. This provides an adequate time frame for all facets of the agreement to be completed. An evaluation process is built into the partnership agreement time-line so that either partner can make appropriate changes when it is time to renew the agreement.

4. How do I initiate a partnership with an organization?

    The CPDG has developed guidelines for the initiation of a partnership. You must evaluate whether or not it meets the following criteria: 1) that the primary interest of the proposal fits with the WRL mission statement; 2) that WRL's values are compatible with the work that will be undertaken; 3) that the proposal contributes to the vision of 2005 and fits the library's strategic direction; 4) that the partnership will benefit the library; 5) that WRL's resources will be utilized reasonably; 6) that you or someone in your department has adequate time to represent the library in developing this partnership; 7) that the time the partnership entails connects to other library activities; 8) that no reasons exist why the library would not want to be involved in the partnership; and, 9) that another group in the community does not do the same thing better.

5. With whom should I discuss the idea?

    You should contact your department head initially and then if she or he approves of your idea, you should discuss the partnership proposal with the community partnership development director to verify that there are no conflicts with pursuing the partnership. For details, see the document, "How to Initiate and Manage a Community Partnership: Engagement or Marriage."

    If your partnership will affect other departments in the library, you should meet with the director of the department for further discussion to see if he/she has adequate resources available to support your proposal.

6. Now that I have received approval from the appropriate parties within WRL, how should I proceed with developing the partnership with the outside organization?

    You should meet with the outside organization to discuss in detail what the goals are of each party to the potential letter of agreement, the ways in which these goals will be met, and what resources will be used to accomplish them. For details, see the document, "How to Initiate and Manage a Community Partnership: Engagement or Marriage."

7. What will my involvement with the CPDG during the initial stages of the partnership be subsequent to my discussion with the outside organization?

    After meeting with the outside organization you will complete a WRL partnership proposal form, which will then be submitted to the CPDG for review. It must meet the criteria enumerated above for the initiation phase of the partnership by the staff member. The library director who makes the approval decision will review the CPDG recommendation.

8. After receiving approval of the partnership proposal by the library director, how should I proceed?

    After consultation with the director of community partnership development, you should draft a partnership letter of agreement that clearly states the partnership's goals and enumerates the responsibilities of each party to accomplish these goals. Examples of partnership agreements, partnership evaluations, and partnership forms are available on the WRL intranet for your review: http://www.wrl.org/staff-only/comm_part/index.html

9. What are the responsibilities of the partnership manager?

    The partnership manager has responsibilities both internally and externally to the partnership. For a details, see the document, "Description of the Roles of Those Involved in the WRL Partnership Program: Engagements and Marriages."

Responsibilities to WRL: manage the day-to-day aspects of the partnership including drafting the partnership proposal and letter of agreement; keeping the community partnership development director updated on changes to the letter of agreement; coordinating publicity and room reservations; and coordinating the evaluation phase.

Responsibilities to the partner: keep the organization's partnership coordinator informed about various aspects of the partnership including publicity, reservations of rooms, coordination of seminars or other educational programs. Work with the partnership coordinator to ensure that the goals enumerated in the letter of agreement timeline are accomplished accordingly.

10.   How are the letters of agreement formatted?

The letter of agreement states the goals of the partnership first. The major project responsibility areas are described in detail. Areas of responsibility include the following: resources that each party will provide to the partnership; facilities that each party will provide or utilize, such as meeting rooms or technical support; promotional pieces and the resources used to create them; evaluation instruments for the partnership and for any programs sponsored by the partnership; program coordinators for each party; and an implementation timeline for the different stages of the partnership.

11.   How do I coordinate any needed publicity for the partnership (e.g. information for the WRL Web page, information for the WRL newsletter, flyers, advertisements etc.)?

The specifics of any publicity for the partnership should be written into the letter of agreement. It is not desirable for the onus to be on the library to use both our graphics design personnel and/or supplies to accomplish the partnership's publicity goals. Instead, sharing of either graphics design personnel or supplies with the partner should be discussed with the potential partner during the partnership agreement phase.

12.   How do I reserve room and technical support?

The Program Services department is developing a web-based interactive program that will enable you to submit room reservations and request technical support online in support of the partnership. Before that system is activated, you should coordinate all room reservations, room configurations, and technical support requests directly through the Program Services department.

13.   How do I evaluate an engagement or marriage with the library?

There is a standard "Evaluating Library Partnerships" form that is utilized by the Williamsburg Regional Library. Both the library partnership coordinator and the partnering agency partnership coordinator complete the form. The evaluation is designed to answer whether the goals that each partner had for the partnership were accomplished and how these goals were realized. The evaluation phase of the partnership is very important because it highlights areas that need improvement or issues that should be resolved through revision of various aspects of the letter of agreement for the subsequent year.

14.   Are partnerships ever dissolved?

It is extremely rare for a partnership to be dissolved. However, if one or both parties in the partnership decide that their needs are no longer being met adequately, the Letter of Agreement will not be renewed. Any issues or concerns about the partnership should be brought to the attention of the partnership manager as soon as possible to prevent dissolution.

Providing access to the various forms used in partnering makes it easy for new managers to incorporate them into their work. Providing access to examples of existing partnership agreements can also be a useful tool for new partnership managers. Looking at the letters of agreement gives the new manager a broad sense of what sort of partnerships the library is interested in pursuing. In addition, the various letters of agreement offer insight into how other library staff members have approached partnering issues. By exploring the details of these various agreements, the new partnership manager can develop a sense of what to include in an agreement with a new community partner and how to address particular issues with community partners, such as publicity, facility use, etc.

A third part of the formal training process for new partnership managers involves shadowing staff who are already managing a partnership. If it is possible, staff new to partnership management can learn a great deal from examining the day-to-day management of an existing partnership. This training can be particularly useful with a new staff member taking over the management of an existing partnership. It will be easier to make the transition from one manager to the next if the new manager can sit in on meetings and participate in the process prior to taking on full responsibilities. However, there will be times when a new manager comes into a partnership without this preparation. At these times, the community partnership development director should be available to support the new manager, even to the point of attending initial meetings and participating in planning if needed.

Some Additional Partnership Management Considerations

Identifying Partnership Managers

The broad skill set outlined in the beginning of this chapter is meant to prepare the new partnership manager to deal with the basics of developing a fruitful relationship with a community partner. Above all, the ability to communicate clearly with both library staff and the staff of the community partner is the most critical contribution to a successful partnership. As a partnership develops, other specific skills become important, depending on the direction of the relationship and of the initiatives associated with the partnership. There are partnerships in which program planning skills are at the forefront. Other partnerships may require the manager to have strong instructional skills. Some partnerships demand more of an ability to work interdepartmentally, coordinating a variety of staff and resources.

In most cases, the staff person who brings a potential partnership idea forward is the person who manages that partnership, at least initially. This is the person who is excited about the possibilities of the relationship, and who, frequently, already has established some sort of relationship with the prospective partner. There may be some situations in which this will not be the case. An idea may be proposed by a staff member who does not have any interest in actually working to develop the relationship. In this case, if the decision is made to proceed with establishing a partnership, a manager should be appointed. A similar case occurs when the manager of an existing partnership leaves the library and a new manager must be assigned to that relationship.

These situations raise a couple of possibilities and questions for the library regarding its approach to partnering. First is the question of whether each public service department should have a designated partnership coordinator. This person would have the responsibility for coordinating partnering opportunities within an individual department, for coordinating specific partnerships (but not necessarily all departmental partnerships), for working with department staff on developing new relationships, and for making partnering part of the departmental planning process. At Williamsburg Regional Library, only the Adult Services Department has designated a specific position to work on partnering. The community services librarian, a senior librarian position, is responsible for coordinating several of the departments' relationships with community partners, and she works with department staff on developing new partnerships. Even with this position in place, individual staff members still can manage any partnership that they wish to develop. But the community services librarian is there to step in when needed; if a partnership manager leaves the library or is incapacitated, the community services librarian has a strong understanding of the partnering process, and can make the transition go more smoothly.

In some instances, the management of the relationship changes as the partnership develops. For example, a partnership that begins with a very small focus may develop into a larger relationship with multiple initiatives. In these cases, the original manager may no longer be the person best qualified to coordinate the partnership. This may be due to time constraints, skills, interests, or to the librarywide nature of the relationship.

As partnerships expand, you may find that coordination of the partnership by a team of library staff is the most effective method of managing the relationship. This happens especially in partnerships that involve multiple initiatives. In these cases, the individual initiatives can be managed by a variety of staff across the institution, depending on which departments are most involved. It is important to still have a central partnership manager who is the main contact person for both the library staff who are managing initiatives and the community partner. Our partnership with the local public school system is managed by a team comprising the community partnership development director, who is the coordinator, and the heads of the Youth Services, Adult Services, and Program Services departments. Individual initiatives within this relationship are carried out by staff in each of these departments. Partnerships that are managed by a team within the library should have an internal communication plan that details how the team will operate. See the communication guidelines (in the box) for an example of a communication plan that we drew up for our library/school partnering team.

Williamsburg Regional Library/Williamsburg-James City County Public Schools Partnership

Communication Guidelines for the Library Department Heads and Staff

The new Williamsburg Regional Library and Williamsburg—James City County Public Schools partnership letter of the agreement sets out goals, initiatives and a framework for our relationship with the school division through the 2004 fiscal year. The community partnership development director will manage the partnership for the library. She will also serve as the library's point person for all communication to and from the library concerning the partnership's goals, framework, and timeline. The directors of the Adult Services, Youth Services and Program Services departments will assist the community partnership development director as members of a Williamsburg Regional Library school partnership team. This team will work with the school division staff through fiscal year 2004 to further establish procedures and standards for a successful relationship.

To ensure good internal communication, library department heads and staff are asked to follow these guidelines when working with public school faculty and staff.

- Library staff should continue to work directly with school staff on initiatives approved and listed in the current partnership letter of agreement. Department heads should notify the community partnership development director of questions or concerns that arise from initiatives as they relate to the partnership goals, procedures, or the timeline. Staff should continue to enter all new contacts with school staff in the Community Relationship Database.

- Departments that would like to try a new initiative that is not part of the current letter of agreement should work through the community partnership development director. The current partnership agreement identifies cooperative initiatives that (a) the library and the school division have agreed upon as a priority, and (b) are available to schools within the division.

- The community partnership development director's role as the partnership manager:

  - Coordinate the library's responsibilities to meet the terms of the letter of agreement and the timeline. To accomplish this, the community partnership development director will work with appropriate library department heads, and/or the library-public school partnership team. The community partnership development director will bring together appropriate library and school division staff. She will communicate concerns and questions to the school division representative as appropriate. She will continue to work with library and school staff division staff to resolve problems and identify opportunities within the partnership. She will keep the library director, the CPDG, the library staff and the library board of trustees informed of the WRL-WJCC Public Schools partnership.

  - The community partnership development director will not manage individual library-school cooperative initiatives.

- The Williamsburg Regional Library School Partnership Team will continue to work with the school division staff to prioritize all cooperative initiatives, to set-up evaluation methods, to develop a model for marketing library programs and services through the schools, and to identify opportunities and issues to address.

In many institutions there is not a specific staff member who has the responsibility for taking on partnership management responsibilities when needed. In these situations, consider the following points when trying to identify a possible partnership manager. One place to look for potential managers is staff who are idea people. They will often be the ones who bring a passion to whatever work they are doing. Every library has these sorts of employees. They may already be in positions in the existing staff structure that lend themselves to partnership management. Outreach coordinators, program coordinators, and school liaisons often will be able to effectively manage community partnerships.

Autonomy Issues

A successful partnership manager brings to the job a blend of passion about the possibilities offered by the relationship and objectivity about the process itself. This blending of passion and objectivity may be the most difficult part of managing a partnership. The partnership manager has a great deal of freedom in developing the relationship and the concomitant responsibility for the success of the partnership. As we have seen, too much personal investment in a partnership can cloud the evaluation of the relationship and keep the manager from making the needed changes, or even ending the relationship if needed.

It is important that all partnership managers understand that they are not autonomous. Partnership managers are associated with a particular library department, and they need to report back to the head of that department on issues with the partnership. The library's community partnership development director serves as a consultant in the partnering process but does not supervise or evaluate staff who are managing partnerships. This can be confusing to new partnership managers, who are working closely with the community partnership development director in establishing a relationship with a community partner. Department heads are responsible for how partnering is used in their departments and must receive clear communication about responsibilities and roles from all partnership managers.

The autonomy issue can also come up from the other direction, when staff, especially paraprofessional staff, who are managing a partnership may feel uncomfortable going directly to the head of another department to deal with cross-departmental partnering issues. There are a variety of ways to deal with this issue, and which way you choose depends on the particular situation and the staff involved. In some cases, it may be most effective for the partnership manager to work through his or her department head in these negotiations. At other times, the community partnership development director can be a facilitator and a mediator between staff from different departments. In any case, careful communication about the partnership and its initiatives is essential to ameliorating these problems.

Compensation Issues

If your library chooses to adopt partnership development as a strategic direction, you must find a way to reward those staff who are responsible for the success of the program, particularly with staff who take on partnership management responsibilities that extend beyond their current duties. Most organizations have a system set up to recognize staff performance, and using these existing compensation mechanisms is often a good way to reward staff for their work in partnership development. Merit pay and similar systems offer supervisors a means to compensate those staff members whose work exceeds expectations.

Other mechanisms for staff recognition include nomination of staff for awards at the local, regional, and national level. These awards do not necessarily have to be in the library field. Often a community partner will be aware of possible awards in his or her areas that can serve to recognize library staff for work in partnership development. As an example, a partnership between the Williamsburg Regional Library and the National Park Service resulted in that particular partnership manager being awarded the Northeast Region Interpretive Volunteer Award from the Park Service. These types of awards not only recognize the individual employees, but they also serve to promote the success of the library's partnering program to library staff, the library board, funding bodies, and other potential partners in the community.

Summary

The library's partnership managers are key players in the library's relationship with the community. Therefore you want to make sure that these people have the skills necessary to represent the library. If partnering is going to be an effective tool for the library in achieving its mission, it makes sense that library administrators look for "partnership qualified" staff when hiring and use the skill set enumerated above as a starting point. Among current staff, look for partnership managers among those staff members who are leaders in their areas. Seek out partnership managers who can balance passion and enthusiasm with objectivity in evaluating their partnerships. Finally, be sure to recognize the work that library partnership managers do, in as many ways as possible, to keep the excitement about partnering alive, and to encourage other staff members to look at partnering possibilities.

9

Partnership Problems

When an institution is approaching community partnering, it is useful to be aware of some of the potential problem areas that exist. Differences between the partners often arise over the course of their association, and you need to address these issues directly. Dealing with small problems in a timely fashion generally prevents them from becoming bigger issues. The relationship developed between the partners is more fragile in the early stages. At least in the initial stages, the partnership relies, a great deal on mutual trust. Failure to address problems as they arise quickly erodes this trust, leaving the relationship on a shaky foundation.

In partnership development, as in most new ventures, there are certain givens that may turn into problems if you are not aware of them and have not prepared for them. If you enter the partnering process understanding these possible sources of problems, you will find it easier to establish procedures for dealing with them. Setting up internal structures for partnering, as discussed in chapter 4, crafting meticulous letters of agreement (chapter 6), and making careful choices of partnership managers helps ameliorate these potential problems.

A Slow Process

The first of these givens in partnering is that the process of developing a partnership tends to be slow. To go back to the marriage analogy, a relationship that is based on clear understandings and considered intentions is more likely to be successful that one that is based on a whirlwind courtship. The same is true for a community partnership. When you are planning a potential partnership, build sufficient time into the process to allow it to flourish. As mentioned in chapter 6 on drafting letters of agreement, be sure to include a timeline for the various aspects of the partnership (specific initiatives, evaluation) in the letter of agreement. In addition, the cross-departmental nature of most community partnerships requires a great deal of transparency in the process. Lots of eyes need to see the proposal and the drafts of letters of agreement. This transparency is a benefit to the process because it makes it easier to deal with concerns and issues before they become major problems, but making sure that everyone is informed and has agreed to support the partnership also takes time.

Relationship Changes

Another given is that relationships change over time. Library staff who are involved in partnering must be open to these changes and not become so emotionally invested in a relationship that they cannot make needed changes. These changes can result from a variety of factors. Most commonly, there is some change of condition in one or both of the partners' situations. These changes frequently are financial, and are often, but not always, related to budget cuts. Loss of funding may mean that an institution needs to re-adjust its priorities, and this may affect how it approaches partnering. At the same time, as we have pointed out, budget cuts may also encourage a community organization to look at existing partnerships as a way to make better use of scarcer resources. So, budget cuts can increase as well as erode interest in partnering.

As organizations develop, their missions may change to keep pace with outside pressures and demands. There may come a time in your existing partnerships when the missions and vision of the two institutions are no longer a good match. At this point, you need to look at what the partnership is accomplishing and determine whether these changes have affected the two organizations' ability to work well together. This does not necessarily mean that the partnership has ended, but it does require that the partners sit down and see if these changes are leading the relationship into new territory, or if they reflect a developing incompatibility.

The possibility of divorce certainly exists in community partnerships. In these cases, you should try to make the ending of the relationship as harmonious as possible. Keep the lines of communication open between the two institutions, as the possibility of a new relationship arising out of the old one will usually exist.

To illustrate this point, the Williamsburg Regional Library established a partnership with a community college in a neighboring community to use our computer lab as a site for computer training classes. The college was looking at ways to expand workforce training and noncredit classes into our area, and we thought that the computer classes would provide two benefits for the library. First, library staffing did not allow us to offer basic computer training to the community, and these classes did just that. Second, the classes would bring a new group of users into the library. The first year, the relationship seemed to work well, but in the second and third years, the college found that fewer students were signing up for these classes, and that classes were frequently being cancelled. From the library's perspective, this was a problem because our computer lab was being booked and then not used. The college felt that they had overextended their class offerings in the area and were not making the best use of resources. So, during the evaluation process both parties decided it would be in their best interests to end this partnership. Although the formal marriage was dissolved, the two organizations continue to look at opportunities to work together in the community. The college is currently planning on developing a physical presence in the Williamsburg community, and we have been discussing how the Williamsburg Regional Library may be a part of that process. The "divorce" was very amicable and has led to the exploration of new opportunities for the former partners.

Staffing Changes

Another given that must be taken into consideration is staffing changes that will occur. In any institution, staff will come and go for a variety of reasons. A library staff person who is involved in managing a partnership leaving the institution presents a particular challenge to the partnership. Community partnerships function well because of the trust between the individuals who are managing the relationship. As discussed in chapter 8, changes in partnership management have the potential to erode this trust-based relationship. Keeping your community partner aware of situations as they develop is essential to keeping the relationship going when there is a staff change on the library's part. Of course, there will be times when a change in management of a partnership becomes necessary to keep the relationship functioning. If the library's partnership manager is not able to adequately carry out the responsibilities of the job, it is important to put a new manager into that position who has the skill set outlined in chapter 8.

There are other issues that can arise over the course of a partnership that may turn into problems if they are not addressed. Some of these issues are examined in earlier chapters as they relate to specific aspects of partnership development. Other possible problems are more general to the concept of partnering. These potential problems fall into two categories—those that may come up between the partners (external problems) and those that may arise within the library (internal problems).

Possible External Problems

Many, if not all, problems that develop between partners arise from a lack of clear communication between the partners. We have stressed the importance of making sure that the letter of agreement for the partnership carefully spells out the roles and responsibilities of each of the partners. Time spent on this step should diminish the possibility for future problems. Nonetheless, we have found that there are certain issues that can arise even with a well-crafted letter of agreement. Awareness of these possible problem areas helps keep the partnership focused. Chapter 5 addresses some of the specific problems encountered when trying to match up missions with a community partner. The following list discusses some other problems that you may face with a community partner:

- **Loss of trust between partners:** Situations can occur that can cause one partner to lose trust in the other (failure to follow through on responsibilities, poor communication, misuse of the relationship). This issue must be addressed immediately, as trust is at the core of the relationship.

- **Shifting missions:** As organizations and libraries grow, their missions and visions evolve. As discussed, this is not inherently a problem, but it is important to ensure that the partnership continues to support the missions of both partners. Regular evaluation of the partnership (see chapter 7 for details) is essential to its success.

- **Inflated expectations for the partnership:** Partnership development is exciting. It offers the library and the community partner new ways to reach out to the community and to continue to remain relevant. This enthusiasm must be tempered with an objective assessment of what the partnership can accomplish. By having the partnership proposal reviewed by a variety of library departments, you increase the likelihood that expectations for the relationship will be kept within the bounds of the do-able. Setting up the internal structures for partnering to allow such reviews (see chapter 4) will help to blend enthusiasm and reality.

- **Partner does not understand the limits of the relationship:** Inflated expectations do not arise only within the library. You will sometimes find that the community partner sees the partnership as a bottomless sack of resources. Again, it is crucial that the letter of agreement clearly spell out what the partners will do, and in particular, what resources they will be providing to the partnership. Be as specific as possible in the letter of agreement—list things such as exactly how many times library facilities can be used by the partner, what sort of promotional space the relationship will get in the library newsletter, and what sorts of limits there will be on technical support for facilities. By setting the limits up front, you make clear to the partner what the library can and cannot do to support the initiatives of the partnership.

- **Different views of the partnering process:** It is easy to assume that your community partner has the same institutional focus on partnering that the library has. However, when working with a partner that is a department or division within a larger institution, you may find that it views partnering as arising out of that particular department or division, not out of the larger institution. This can lead to communication problems, as the library may assume that all issues relating to working with the other institution flow through the partnership, whereas the partner sees the relationship in a much narrower way. Be sure that you understand how the community partner views the overall partnering process as you enter the relationship.

- **Promotion of the partnership:** Promoting the partnering relationship is an area where problems may develop. Because this is the point at which both institutions are putting themselves directly in the public eye, it is essential that both partners are in agreement on how publicity is to be handled. It is not only embarrassing when a news release or poster is put out that contains the wrong name for one of the partners or misinformation about a program, it also calls into question the seriousness of the partnership. Fortunately, this is an issue that should be easy to deal with, by including a review clause for all partnership-related publicity in the letter of agreement. Each partner should have the opportunity to preview any information that includes its name or logo and is related to the activities of the partnership.

- **Loss of energy or focus or unforeseen events:** There will be times when a formerly productive partnership begins to stagnate. Neither partner is pushing the relationship, and there does not seem to be any energy directed at new initiatives. This may occur when the partnership manager leaves one of the institutions, when a new director comes into one of the institutions and does not feel strongly about partnerships, or when some unusual circumstance occurs that shifts one institution's focus. For example, in 2003 Hurricane Isabel caused substantial damage to the property of two of our community partners in Williamsburg. These partnerships will be on hold until the partner is able to regroup from this incident. Again, the evaluation process comes into play here, and if the partnership managers are objective about the relationship, perhaps this partnership should be ended. However, the evaluation process may also indicate that the partnership has fulfilled its initial mission, and that the partners need to look for new directions for the relationship.

- **Partnership is based on mistaken assumptions:** You may find after you have entered a relationship that some of the basic assumptions you made about opportunities offered by the community partner are incorrect. This can occur even when you have been careful in trying to match missions with the partner (see chapter 5 for information on exploring the community and developing relationships). For example, you may establish a partnership because you anticipate that the relationship will give you access to a large population that you are not currently reaching. After you get into the partnership, you may discover that in reality the partner was not as connected to this community as you had thought. While this discovery would be disappointing, it would not necessarily develop into a larger problem if the partnership meets one or more of the other reasons you have established as the focus for partnering. This situation can become a problem if it creates bigger issues such as a loss of trust between the partners.

- **Lack of authority:** It will be difficult to have a fruitful partnership if the community partner's partnership manager does not have the authority to make decisions at some level for that institution. When you are establishing a partnership, make sure that you are dealing with staff from the partnering organization who can make decisions about issues that will affect the relationship. This does not necessarily mean that you always need to be dealing with the head of the organization. But it will be difficult to carry out partnership initiatives without the authority to actually do them.

Challenges to Partnering with Businesses

There are some issues that are particularly common in working on partnerships with businesses. While partnerships with for-profits can be rewarding, they do present challenges that are not as often faced in working with nonprofits or governmental institutions.

- **It's harder to match missions:** Businesses exist to make money. The mission of any for-profit organization is to be a financial success. It can be a challenge to find areas where the library's mission can match up with that of the business. Look for locally owned businesses or those that have displayed a strong long-term commitment to supporting their communities, as these will be more likely matches for the library. Above all, the library cannot allow itself to simply be used to promote the products of a particular business.

- **Control issues:** Often, businesses have less local control over their decisions. Partnership efforts may be slowed or buried in the effort to go through lots of layers to get approval of initiatives, publicity, and funding. Be aware that partnerships with businesses may require even more patience than other partnerships.

- **Image problems:** Business images may change rapidly in response to perceived needs, and often these changes are outside the control of the local institution. A major corporate scandal may not involve the local branch of a business, but the image of that organization in the community will be affected by these sorts of issues. The library needs to be aware of how its partnership with a for-profit institution will reflect on the library's name in the community.

- **Choosing among businesses:** The library also must be careful that in developing a partnership with a local business it is not seen as promoting that organization over its local competitors. If you establish a partnership with a local grocery store, other similar stores may approach you wanting to set up partnerships also. You need to be prepared to say no to partnerships that do not meet your needs, but at the same time be sensitive to not promoting one local business over another.

- **Differences in corporate culture:** Businesses generally operate under different decision-making processes, corporate vocabularies, timetables, and ways of measuring success than libraries. When you look at establishing a relationship with a for-profit, you must take these factors into account, and plan accordingly.

Possible Internal Problems

In addition to problems that can arise between partners, partnership development can be affected by issues that arise within the library. These issues can create a climate in the institution that makes it difficult for partnership development to occur.

- **Director does not see value of partnering:** If you cannot convince the director of the library that partnership development is a valuable tool for future success, it will be impossible to develop meaningful relationships with outside organizations. Partnership development requires the library to commit staff resources and time to developing relationships. If the director is not willing to make these commitments, you should not be looking for community partnerships.

- **Library staff does not understand partnering:** To have a successful partnering program at the library, there has to be a core group of library staff who understand what partnering is and how it differs from traditional library outreach. We have discussed in previous chapters the importance of involving all staff in laying the foundation for partnership development through creating a strategic plan and through making partnering a strategic direction for the library. Educating staff first about the value of partnerships to the success of the library, and then about the mechanisms of developing specific partnerships, is essential to the success of the partnering program.

- **Departmental territoriality:** As we have pointed out, most community partnerships cross library departmental lines. If the library does not emphasize the importance of staff working cross-departmentally, partnership opportunities will be limited to those small relationships that can be contained within a single department. Library administration must create a culture that breaks down territoriality and encourages staff from all departments to think and act collaboratively.

- **Community knowledge is not shared within the library:** This item relates to the previous issue of departmental territoriality. Successful partnership development requires that all library departments be aware of what other library staff are doing in the community. Setting up communication mechanisms such as a database of community contacts will help with this issue, but only if it is used and updated by all departments. It can be disconcerting for a library partnership manager to discover that the partner with whom he or she is working has had a long-term relationship with another library department that the manager was unaware of. Situations such as this reflect poorly on the library in the eyes of existing and potential community partners.

- **Focusing solely on the formal partnerships:** While we have almost exclusively discussed marriages and engagements in this book, it is important to remember that the majority of library partnerships with community organizations will be in the form of a date or a glance. While these interactions may not be as high profile as a formal marriage with a community partner, they are essential to the continued success of the library and its partnering program. These initial contacts in the community may lay the groundwork for future expanded partnerships. Don't neglect to keep up with these smaller or more casual relationships.

- **Librarians' accommodating nature:** One thing to keep in mind when negotiating with a potential community partner is the tendency of librarians to be accommodating. After all, we seek to provide the best service possible to our users and try to help as much as we can. Too often, we are willing to give our time and resources to someone without expecting a return. Partnerships look for commitments from both partners and are only successful when they are mutually beneficial.

- **Not choosing carefully:** If a library takes on too many partnerships, or is unwilling to terminate unsuccessful relationships, the entire partnership program suffers. Not only do the problem partnerships waste staff time and energy, but other, potentially successful relationships do not get the attention they need. Prioritize your partnering prospects and make sure that they fit in with what you can realistically do.

Although you cannot anticipate all the possible problems that may occur as you begin to develop community partnerships, an awareness of some of the potential difficulties will help you to deal with them when they arise.

10 Conclusions

Partnership development offers libraries an exciting tool to integrate themselves into their communities and to remain relevant in the twenty-first century. It is a tool that can be used by any library that is willing to put in the effort to build fruitful relationships with organizations and businesses in the community. At the Williamsburg Regional Library, partnering has become an important tool for carrying out our mission. We use both our formal partnerships—marriages and engagements—and our informal community contacts—glances and dates—to enhance the services we offer and to expand our reach into the community.

We hope that the processes and procedures we have described here give your library a foundation for building formal, long-term relationships with local government, nonprofit, and for-profit institutions. We see these sorts of associations as beneficial not only to the two partnering organizations but also to the community that they serve.

As libraries continue to strive to provide the best service possible to their patrons and to justify their existence to their funding bodies, partnerships offer an attractive opportunity to work collaboratively with those members of the community who share the same mission and vision. To reiterate the six reasons why libraries should consider developing community partnerships:

- To reach new library users

- To reach current library users in a new way

- To tap into community assets and strengths

- To gain support for library resources and/or programs

- To gain valuable community feedback

- To create new resources

We encourage you to look at your library's existing relationships with community organizations to determine whether your library is benefiting from these associations as much as it should. Too often libraries are willing to give much and ask little in return. Partnering offers a new direction, a venture in which both the library and its community partner share the risks and rewards of working together to support their missions. Partnering offers those willing to make the effort a valuable mechanism to be successful in the coming years.

Bibliography:
Further Readings on Partnering

Albanese, Andrew, et al. "Waco-McLennan County Library System." *Library Journal* 127 (December 2002): 24.

Anft, Michael. "Toward Corporate Change." *The Chronicle of Philanthropy* 14 (September 19, 2002): 9.

Austin, James E. *The Collaborative Challenge: How Non-profits and Businesses Succeed Through Strategic Alliances.* San Francisco: Jossey-Bass, 2000.

Chobot, Mary C., and Jean Preer. "Partnerships to Promote Literacy: A National Program Helps Libraries Join Forces with Local Organizations to Boost Community Support." *American Libraries* 22 (March 1991): 256–58.

Durrance, Joan C., and Karen Fisher. *How Libraries and Librarians Help: Outcome-Based Evaluation Toolkit.* Available at http://www.si.umich.edu/libhelp/toolkit/index.html (accessed April 1, 2003).

Goldberg, Susan. "Community Action Now: Defying the Doomsayers." *Library Journal* 118 (March 15, 1993): 29.

Holt, Glen E. "Public Library Partnerships: Mission Driven Tools for 21st Century Success." Available at http://www.internationales-netzwerk.de/en/x_media/pdf/holt6en.pdf (accessed May 2, 2004).

Linden, Russell M. *Working Across Boundaries: Making Collaboration Work in Government and Nonprofit Organizations.* San Francisco: Jossey-Bass, 2002.

McDougal, Paul. "Collaborative Business." *Information Week* 836 (May 7, 2001): 42.

Oder, Norman. "Three PLs Get Grants from IMLS." *Library Journal* 124 (October 15, 1999): 22.

Reiss, Alvin H. "Partnerships a Key to Future Arts Development." *Fund Raising Management* 32 (July 2001): 33.

Sagawa, Shirley, and Eli Segal. *Common Interest, Common Good: Creating Value Through Business and Social Sector Partnerships.* Boston: Harvard Business School Press, 2000.

Whelan, David. "Rethinking Nonprofit Partnerships." *Chronicle of Philanthropy* 14 (June 27, 2002): 36.

Index

About the Authors

Janet L. Crowther is the Director of Community Partnership Development at the Williamsburg (VA) Regional Library. She received her MSLS from the Catholic University of America School of Library and Information Science in 1981. Janet has worked as a reference librarian, a legal librarian, and as a field consultant for the Idaho State Library.

Barry Trott is Adult Services Director at the Williamsburg (VA) Regional Library. He received his MSLS from the Catholic University of America School of Library and Information Science in 1997. He has worked as a reference librarian and as Readers' Services librarian, and is chair of the RUSA/CODES Readers' Advisory Committee.